THE ROLE AND
MINISTRY
OF WOMEN

Also available in the Pioneer *Perspectives* series:

Prophecy in the Church   Martin Scott

For further information on the Pioneer *Perspectives* series and Pioneer, please write to: P.O. Box 79c, Esher, Surrey, KT10 9LP

THE ROLE AND MINISTRY OF WOMEN

Martin Scott

THE ROLE AND MINISTRY OF WOMEN

© Pioneer 1992.

Published by Word (UK) Ltd. / Pioneer 1992.

ISBN   0-85009-725-8   (Australia ISBN 1-86258-195-9)

Unless otherwise indicated, Scripture quotations are from the HOLY BIBLE, NEW INTERNATIONAL VERSION (NIV). Copyright © 1973, 1978, 1984 by International Bible Society.

Front cover illustration: *Girl Reading,* Renoir, courtesy of Musée D'Orsay, Paris. Giraudon/Bridgeman Art Library.

Reproduced, printed and bound in Great Britain for Word (UK) Ltd. by Clays Ltd., St Ives plc.

92 93 94 95 / 10 9 8 7 6 5 4 3 2 1

FOREWORD

Pioneer *Perspectives* are perhaps more than their title suggests!

They are carefully researched presentations of material, on important issues, appealing to thinking churches, creative leaders and responsible Christians.

Each *Perspective* pioneers in as much as it is at the cutting edge of biblical and theological issues. Each will continue to pioneer with new ideas, concepts and data drawn from Scripture, history and a contemporary understanding of both.

They are perspectives in as much as they aim to be an important contribution to the ongoing debate on issues such as women in ministry and leadership; prophets and prophecy in the church; biblical models of evangelism; integrating and discipling new believers; growing and building local churches and further perspectives on Christ's second coming.

Importantly, these studies use a journal style of presentation, and are written by people who are currently working out the implications of the issues they are writing about, in local churches. This is vital if we are to escape the dangerous fantasy of abstract theology without practical experience. They are not written to contribute to the paralysis of analysis—rather to feed, strengthen, nurture and inform so that we can be equipped to get God's will done, by networking the nations with the Gospel using all the resources that are available to us.

God's Word is always an event. How much we thank Him that He has left us an orderly account of what He wants us to believe, how He wants us to live, and what He wants us to do in order to bring heaven to the earth. As we embrace a better understanding of Scripture, rooted in local church, national and international mission, we shall become a part of the great eschatological purpose of bringing back the King—not for a church defeated, cowering and retiring but for one which, despite colossal odds, pressures and persecutions, is faithful to her Lord and His word. To do that we must 'search the Scriptures' to see if many of these 'new things' are true. I commend these *Perspectives* to you as they are published on a regular basis throughout these coming years.

Gerald Coates
Director Pioneer Trust/Team Leader

ACKNOWLEDGEMENTS

With thanks to all in Cobham who have shown me total acceptance and have believed in me—particularly to my wife Sue, Gerald Coates and Steve Clifford (two good friends and colleagues), and, finally, to two great children —Benjamin and Judith.

With respect to this particular subject I want to acknowledge and thank Roger Forster for his input. It was he who first opened my eyes to the nature of the subject and shed light on various relevant portions of Scripture.

With regard to the editing of this volume I want to thank Christine Leonard who gave some very useful input and perspectives, but particularly Chris Bourne who gave many hours to the hard work of making this book readable.

Martin Scott
July 1991

Pioneer consists of a team and network of churches, committed to dynamic and effective biblical Christianity.

The national team act as advisers and consultants to churches, which in many cases develop into a partnership with the Pioneer team. These are the churches keen to identify with the theology, philosophy, ethos and purpose of Pioneer. The team have a vigorous youth ministry, church-planting strategy and evangelistic emphasis.

Training courses include Equipped to Lead, Emerging Leaders and the highly successful TIE teams (Training In Evangelism).

Pioneer have also been instrumental in initiating and funding March for Jesus (with Ichthus/YWAM); Jubilee Campaign (for the suffering church worldwide); and ACET (Aids Care Education Training).

CONTENTS

PREFACE

This book is the result of a number of months of reading, study and discussion. I have sought to be faithful to the teaching of Scripture with regard to the subject of women in the church and specifically of women in leadership. I cannot claim that this study is exhaustive or that it is entirely original. I have been stimulated in my own thinking both by those who are in favour of women in leadership, and also by those who take the opposing position.

This is a subject which has come to the fore in recent years. There has been much heated debate and, as a result, views tend to be extreme on this matter. There is, on the one hand, the fear of compromising Scripture, of falling into the unbiblical trap of emulating the trends we see in the Western world. On the other hand there is the passionate appeal that we must not leave women unfulfilled and in bondage, when the Gospel is to bring freedom to all who have received the life of the Holy Spirit through the death of Christ.

In approaching the Scriptures we need to have a dynamic approach which will enable us to interpret them in the light of their culture and background. If we fail to recognise the need for this, we could well end up falling into the same trap as a previous generation of evangelicals, who were opposed to the abolition of slavery on the grounds of the biblical evidence. On the other hand we need to ensure that we are being faithful to the teaching of Scripture and not removing boundaries which God has set in place. If we ignore this warning we could end up opening up a door, for instance, to homosexuality, claiming that Paul and the other writers were speaking purely into their own culture. If we reduce everything to 'that was the culture then', we are making culture, rather than the revelation of God in Scripture, the touchstone of truth.

Rather than begin with the direct teaching of Scripture on this subject it would seem better to lay a foundation with regard to some wider biblical issues. Much of the teaching on the role of women centres around the issue of authority. Questions are often raised, such as what authority may a woman exercise? Or whose authority should she be under? Therefore it would seem good first of all to define the nature of authority in Scripture. The converse of authority is seen as submission (often wrongly described as subjection) so our initial line of approach will be to look at these two areas.

PART ONE

CHAPTER 1

AUTHORITY AND SUBMISSION

1.1 Introduction

Authority and submission can be very emotive subjects. Most, if not all of us, have experienced 'authority' which has been corrupted by personal vanity and ambition. Many people, when they hear the word, feel an immediate response of either fear or anger, depending on whether they have a strong or weak reaction to those who would dominate and intimidate them. Authority speaks to them of the theft of freedom, rights and individuality. The word 'submission' speaks to them of personal loss; it raises fears of abuse.

We must understand that these reactions, which are far more common than you might think, need to be brought into the light of God's love. The first point is that the thing that is wrong here is the corrupted use of authority. These reactions do not mean that the person is harbouring a rebellious attitude. Indeed, in extreme cases, a bit of 'rebellion' against abuse is necessary for self-defence. Authority is never owned independently. Nobody has authority in and of himself. And all who exercise authority are accountable to the one person who does have authority in Himself. He is the one person who can safely be trusted with that authority because His will is good and perfect and acceptable.

All human authority is derived from God's authority and it is exercised by His permission. It is drawn from His right and delegated by Him; entrusted to human society to be used according to His will. God holds accountable all who exercise authority, from the ruler of a nation to the father and mother in the home. And there will be judgement on how that authority was used.

To be in authority means to have a clear mandate and responsibility to lead, guide and inspire all who should be under that authority. The fact that someone exercises authority does not place them beyond correction—far from it; Jesus reserved His strongest words for those in positions of leadership.

The purpose of this section is to set out a description of what authority is for and what it is to be like in terms of a biblical outlook. We need to be willing to let go some of our misconceptions and prejudices. The answer to abused authority is not anarchy, it is God's authority used in God's way.

1.1.1 Authority—to serve people

Authority in God's kingdom is of a totally different order from authority outside of Christ. Jesus made this clear when He said:

> You know that those who are regarded as rulers of the Gentiles lord it over them, and their high officials exercise authority over them. Not so with you. Instead, whoever wants to become great among you must be your servant, and whoever wants to be first must be slave of all. For even the Son of Man did not come to be served but to serve, and to give his life a ransom for many.
>
> (Mark 10:42–45)

Outside of Christ, man's approach to authority tends to be authoritarian: that is, it tends to be about control and imposition. In Christ our authority is to serve people. So Paul says in 2 Corinthians 13:10 that his authority was to build the church up—to promote them rather than 'lord it' over them. Likewise Peter exhorts elders to serve the flock, not by 'lording it' over them, but by being examples to them (1 Peter 5:1–4).

Leadership, in whatever sphere, has authority. Leaders

are also held accountable by God for how they use their authority. It can be abused through 'lording it' over people but this is far removed from the spirit of Christ. We can safely say that any authority which tries to dominate or intimidate people is an illegitimate authority as far as the kingdom of God is concerned.

1.1.2 Authority—over the works of the devil
One example of the authority which Jesus gives to His disciples is found in Luke 10:18 where He says:

> I have given you authority to trample on snakes and scorpions and to overcome all the power of the enemy; nothing [in any way] will harm you.

Our authority is therefore over the works of the enemy, not over people.

We have been given, through the resurrection of Jesus, everything we need to get our mission accomplished. Jesus announced that 'All authority in heaven and on earth' had been first given to Him, and then delegated to us so that we might go in that authority to the ends of the earth with the Gospel. This authority is clearly 'in God' to pull down the kingdom of darkness and set people free from the bondage of Satan. So our authority is over the things that bind people, not over the people themselves. This latter kind of authority is itself a work of darkness. (Perhaps this domineering authority over people would be termed 'witchcraft' by Paul, as there is the same desire to control and manipulate others as is found in the occult practice of witchcraft.) [1]

1.1.3 Authority—flows from being in submission
Luke. 7:1–10 is the story of the centurion who recognised that Jesus moved in authority because, like himself, He was submitted to authority.

If we want to move in authority, for legitimate purposes, then we need to place ourselves under authority. There are no hierarchies where we can get to the top of the pyramid and so reach a position where we do not need to be under authority. Ultimately we are under God's authority but this is 'made flesh' as we submit to the spirit of Christ which is revealed in His people, the church. Paul says we are to, 'Submit to one another out of reverence for Christ' (Eph. 5:21).

1.1.4 Submission—a command for all believers

Nowhere are those in authority told to 'subject' those who are under them. Rather those who are under authority are told to 'submit' themselves. (The Greek consistently uses the middle voice which must always be translated as 'submit yourselves'.)

No believer is allowed exemption from having a submissive attitude. Equality is certainly a myth, but any concept of a hierarchy is repugnant to the spirit of the Gospel which comes to release all believers into servanthood.

So we conclude that no one is allowed to be insubmissive in heart, nor is anyone allowed to lord it over anyone else. This is the framework within which we can explore and think through the relationship between men and women. These attitudes are the key to the harmony of relationships—and the presence of the spirit of Christ is vital to ensure that they are maintained.

From here we will look at specific teaching within Scripture on the subject of authority. We will consider the various spheres of authority and how they interrelate, in order to begin to provide a framework for further discussion.

1.2 Seven realms of authority

All authority resides in God. However, He has delegated some of that authority into the human sphere. As we look through Scripture, I believe that we will find that there are distinct spheres of delegated authority. I am sure it is possible to list these spheres in a way which differs from that below, but I hope that it will be sufficiently clear for our purposes to follow the list as I give it.

The spheres of authority are as follows:

1. God Himself
2. God's Word
3. Conscience
4. The government
5. The employer
6. The church
7. The home

The first three that are listed must never be violated. The first two of these are absolute and require absolute obedience. The third sphere of authority, the conscience, is not absolute—but it is also never to be violated. The final four spheres are spheres of delegated authority and are not absolute—in other words those exercising authority within those spheres can never demand absolute obedience.

We will look at these spheres briefly under their separate headings below. Principles brought out here will help in determining how we will interpret the two final spheres of authority (church and home) with particular reference to men and women. Again, we need to bear in mind the comments we made with regard to authority and submission in the previous section.

1.2.1 God Himself
A Christian starting point must be that God has absolute authority and rules over all. He uses His sovereign authority for our good, to work all things according to His purpose. He alone can demand absolute obedience—rebellion against His authority must be put aside before we even enter the kingdom of heaven. God also delegates authority—so rebellion against His delegated authority is seen as rebellion against God Himself. Rebellion is obviously the opposite attitude to submission.

1.2.2 God's Word
God's word is final and is never to be violated. If God says something, then that settles it. There may be questions with regard to interpretation of Scripture, but its authority is beyond question. There are unclear passages over which we need to retain an open mind—but this is not the same

thing as refusing to accept the clear teachings of Scripture.

With regard to the 'difficult passages' on the role of women, there are different interpretations. If we retain an open mind on these passages, we need to realise that this does not place us in the same category as those who deny clear, revealed truth.

1.2.3 Conscience

We are to keep a good conscience before God and men (e.g. Acts 24:16). We are not to violate our conscience and we can clearly say that the personal conscience is of a higher authority than the edicts of men. Where there is a conflict between whether to obey man or God, there can be only one option—which is to obey God.

We do need to realise that the conscience is not infallible and it needs educating. Conscience is conditioned through culture, upbringing, personality and experience. It therefore needs exposure to the Holy Spirit, Scripture and those with wise, godly counsel.

We would place the authority of the conscience over and above the remaining four delegated realms. But the authority of God and His Word would be placed above the level of the conscience. Again, we can say that the conscience is often the means by which we understand how to implement God's absolute authority in our relationships.

We can summarise the realms and our responses as follows:

1. God and His Word are infallible and demand total obedience.
2. The conscience is not infallible and is in need of education but is not to be violated.
3. With regard to the four realms of human authority which we are yet to look at, we can make the following statements at this stage. We are to submit within the four realms of delegated human authority but we cannot give absolute obedience to anyone within any of these realms. Over any matter of conflict God, His Word and our conscience must take precedence.

Excursus: an introduction to the final four realms of authority

Each realm described covers an independent aspect of human life and relationships. The authority in these realms is to be seen as delegated authority—therefore the one in authority has to answer to God for how that authority is used.

These realms are independent of one another. Someone in authority in one realm is not automatically in authority in another, and cannot simply transfer their authority over to another sphere. For instance, someone in authority at work is not automatically in authority in the church.

However, there is a mutual appeal to the truth which needs to be an influence on those in authority. If we take the example of a person in authority at work coming into the church, we will see how this works out. If this person is unhappy about some aspect of church life he can appeal to the truth and ask that those in authority in the church reconsider what they are doing. He cannot come and legislate what is done, however, as this is not his sphere of authority.

Absolute obedience cannot be required by any of these authorities—this is owed to God alone. So the person in submission is not to do something immoral and then blame the person in authority for pushing them into it. Each person will give an account for their own life before God (Rom. 14:10–12).

We can now go on to look at these final four realms of authority, bearing in mind what we have stated above.

1.2.4 The government

Scriptures: Romans 13:1–7; 1 Peter 2:13–17.

This realm is fairly self-evident. However, by using it as an example, we can illustrate the principle of the independence of each realm. For instance, were a church leader to give an edict which was anti-government, people would not be exempt from prosecution on the basis that they were obeying their leader. So, if a church leader instructs the flock that they are no longer to pay their taxes, this does not mean, when the government finally catches up with them, that only the leader is prosecuted. Each person is to obey the government, regardless of the other authorities he is also under.

1.2.5 The employer
Scriptures: Colossians 3:22—4:1; Ephesians 5:22—6:9; 1 Peter 2:18 (in Scripture this is the master/slave relationship).

The employee is to work for their employer 'as unto the Lord'. This means being faithful, hard-working and following the rules of the employer (with the proviso, as in all these relationships, that only God commands absolute obedience).

1.2.6 The church
Scriptures: Hebrews 13:17; Romans 12:8.

The church has authority within its own sphere. It is not here to have authority over the government, the employer, or the home—as we shall see later. Those in authority in the body of Christ must be mature and must handle the authority which is delegated to them as Christ would— by being examples and laying down their lives for the flock.

Again, it might be helpful to illustrate the independence of these spheres of authority by giving a possible scenario of interaction between the work and the church sphere. If an elder was employed by someone from within his flock, then that elder would be in submission to his employer in the work sphere. He could not say, 'Because I am your elder I will decide how often I come into work, how much I am paid and how much holiday time I will have.' Conversely the employer could not enter the sphere of the church and declare, 'I employ you—therefore I am going to decide how many house-groups we should have, or when and how we are going to meet as a church.'

Each person has authority within their own sphere and cannot legislate over the other's sphere—the spheres are independent. It is also true that, in the kingdom of God, the above picture can work without strain. Both employer and church leader know that they have a Master and that both answer to Him over how they use their authority.

The illustration above, I hope, illustrates the principle of independence. It is necessary to establish this principle at this point, as I believe it carries through into the final realm of authority (the husband–wife relationship). It is important that we lay this foundation because the final realm can be emotive and is particularly so when we look at women in positions of leadership within the church.

1.2.7 The home
Scriptures: Ephesians 5:22—6:4 and Colossians 3:18–21 (parallel passages); 1 Peter 3:1–6.

This is in two areas: children to parents and wives to husbands. It is clear from Scripture that fathers should have a key role in the bringing up of children—indeed only the father is mentioned by Paul in these passages! This at least argues against the bringing up of the children being left to the mother as one of her tasks.

The area which is of particular interest within this book though, is that of the husband/wife relationship. From the passages listed it is clear that wives are asked to submit to their husbands. This is not to preclude the need for the couple as 'one flesh' to submit to the Lord, neither does it exclude the need for the husband to submit to the wife when she is bringing direction from the Lord.

We can leave the question of the meaning of 'head' for the time being but we do need to answer the question which is often raised, namely, 'Is this edict merely cultural and temporal?' In other words, were these instructions given 'for the sake of the Gospel'—i. e. in order not to give offence within their culture?[2]

Was submission of the wife to the husband purely expedient and cultural? We do need to remember that, although Paul sowed the seeds which would eventually abolish slavery, he did not himself advocate the abolition of slavery. So Paul did speak within his own culture and we will need to remember this fact.

I, however, do not believe that this is a purely cultural expression of the relationship, as Paul compares the marriage relationship to that of the relationship between Christ and the church. To say it is cultural in the light of his arguments would be to say that Paul was mistaken and would then cause us to question the authority of Scripture. This then opens the door to other possibilities—e.g. was Paul mistaken over homosexuality?

Paul outlines the need for the wife to submit to authority, as found in her relationship with her own husband. However, this is counterbalanced by the husband's response to his wife being one of sacrificial love. In the same way that Jesus left His Father's home looking for a bride, so the husband leaves his parents' home seeking his bride. Again we need to remember that scriptural authority does not lord it over others but serves them.

We will study the biblical use of the word 'head' in detail at a later stage but it is worth quoting from Gretchen Hull at this stage. In her book *Equal to Serve* she writes, 'The Apostles themselves describe the role of the head in such a way that in practice it makes no difference whether head represents an empowered figure or a source figure.'[3]

With regard to the issue of 'head', we note that God is the head of Christ. If head does carry connotations of authority, then we need to ask how this applies within the Trinity (God is the head of Christ). It certainly does not imply an inequality. Nor are we to understand that there is ever a conflict over wills within the Godhead. This is important, as the only model we have for relationships is the Trinity.

1.3 Interim conclusion—Can women be in authority in the church?

This is a conclusion based purely on the above model and does not take into account the other Scriptures which will be looked at later in depth.

The wife is asked to submit to her husband in the sphere of her marriage. In the church we submit to those in leadership who are God's delegated authorities. Delegation of authority in the home is to the marriage partners but within this there is a primary responsibility given to the husband. Leadership in the home is, in one sense, based on gender, although the parents are to act in unity and as a team. Leadership in the church is based on anointing, not gender.

Let us now look at a practical illustration. We saw the independence of the spheres of authority above using the employer–elder relationship. This time we will look at the illustration in a slightly different form. For the employer we will substitute the husband and we will now take the elder in this illustration to be his wife. So, to expand on the above situation, we would have the wife in authority within the sphere of the church (with the husband submitting to her because she is part of the leadership team) while the husband would be in authority within the home (with the wife following his lead in the context of the marriage).

We do need to bear in mind that we are drawing some artificially distinct lines here—in reality the husband and wife would work together as a team. However, the point that I am making is that if we are not clear which delegated authority we are operating under in a given context, then chaos results.

Despite any practical difficulties or personal insecurities which might surface, we need to recognise that, in the Lord, the scenario that I have given is at least a possibility. This is due to the fact that we all submit to the Lord and also to one another, out of reverence for the Lord.

The above scenario could only work with authority as understood in the Bible—servant authority—and with those who are mature. This I believe is one of the challenges of releasing women into ministry. It would only be possible through the radical liberation of the Gospel—a liberation for women and a liberation for everyone from insecurity.

We could give another possible example in a less theological, or possibly less emotive area. Suppose a husband and wife both work for the same company. Let us assume that the wife is in a senior position to the husband and that he is directly accountable to her. It would therefore follow that in the work situation he would submit to her as his boss, but at home she would submit to him as her husband. Again we are drawing some artificial lines—marriage is not, or at least should not be, a business relationship. Also the illustration wrongly emphasises the independence of the husband—in reality he and his wife are one flesh.

However artificial these illustrations are, I believe once we see realms of authority as distinct and covering independent spheres, it is possible to see how women can operate with as full an authority as any man in the sphere of the church. The above illustrations have used extreme examples—a married woman in authority over her husband in certain situations, because she was in leadership while her husband was not. I would suggest that, if the illustration I have used is possible, then the release of women who are single, or whose husbands are involved with them in church leadership, would be far more straightforward.

Also, we must not reject the possibility of leadership by women simply because it gives us difficulties in seeing how it would work at a practical level. We must only reject the idea if it is found to be unbiblical. This latter issue will be taken up at a later stage in the discussion.

1.4 Do all women need to submit to men?

If it were true that all women must submit to all men we would be dealing with a very big truth. It would be an immutable law, a universal ordering of things based on gender alone. Women would have to submit because they are female and men would rule because they are male. But this would not be an expression of authority in the biblical sense as we have just seen. It would be an expression of rank or seniority and inevitably it would be expressed in one-sided service and disproportionate privilege. If this were the case we should never expect to see women in any form of authority because, historically, authority is not delegated to inferior classes of being; tasks might be delegated, even responsibility might be delegated, but the real authority would be retained. But mothers do have authority over their children, we do have women teachers, we do have women in the police force and in the military.

And we do have a Queen and, until recently, a woman Prime Minister. If authority is determined by gender then we will have to decide what all these things mean.

More importantly, if there is a universal ordering on the basis of gender, we should expect that Scripture would not show a single approving instance of a female exercising authority. Later we will see some of these 'unexpected' instances. If an immutable law were in force, it would be at least as clearly and definitively stated as any of the other principles of God's will, and we would see it enforced every bit as rigorously as any other law. But it is clear that authority is handled in Scripture according to purpose and according to situation.

Even within the marriage relationship (where I do argue for a primary responsibility resting on the husband), it would seem absurd to suggest that there is a rigid order based on gender. In every marriage there are areas where the husband submits to the wife; where she is simply far better equipped and has greater ability than he. Some would argue that in these instances her 'authority' is delegated by the husband and that, in fact, he is not really submitting at all. While this does sound rather like a pretence to protect some sort of pride, there is really no escaping the result. He does submit no matter how much huff and puff goes into the explanation. But if this argument is maintained then we had better be aware of the consequence. If a wife's authorities are always delegated by the husband, and if women in society receive their authority from the men in society (an unsupportable notion) then we have to be able to argue that no woman receives authority for anything from God Himself. What are we to do with this passage ? 'But to as many as did receive . . . Him, He gave the authority[power, privilege, right] to become the children of God.' (John 1:12 Amplified Bible). Surely this describes not the least but the greatest authority ever delegated.

We have established that authority is not inherent. Nobody has authority in and of himself. We have established that authority is measured not by the number of people who have to do as you say, but by the degree to which your authority fulfils the purposes of God. We have also established that authority is for the sake of those who are under it.

Still there is a teaching that all women need to be in submission to all men and it is often taken to include single women. As we come to look at this matter we need to bear in mind the teaching on authority and submission which we have already looked at. Kingdom authority is there to serve others, not to lord it over them. Also, all believers, regardless of gender, are to be submissive in heart—in other words it is not a case of women having to submit to men, while men are allowed to be rebellious and independent.

There are explicit Scriptures which instruct wives to be submissive to their husbands. We will list these below with minimal comment.

1 Corinthians 14:34–35—Women (or wives—same Greek word) are to be in submission and to ask questions of their own husbands at home.

This does not necessarily mean that Paul is exhorting women to submit to the men present, nor even to their own husbands. It is more likely to be a reference to submission to the assembled body. However, wives are instructed to ask their own husbands at home to answer their questions. This passage will be looked at in greater detail in a later section.

Ephesians 5:22—Wives are to submit to their own husbands.

Titus 2:5—Younger wives are to be taught to submit to their own husbands.

1 Peter 3:1—Wives in the same way are to be subject to their own husbands.

We take these Scriptures together because they all clearly refer to the marriage relationship. All of the above use a very explicit Greek phrase (*tois idiois andrasin*—'to their own husbands'). In other words they are not saying that all women must submit to all men, or to all married men—but that wives are to submit to their own husbands. Note this does not mean that a husband can lord it over his wife, nor that he is encouraged to be insubmissive in heart toward her or anyone else. It would, however, appear to say that there is a greater responsibility placed upon the husband to be the initiator in seeking to lead them as one flesh in their walk with the Lord and in the discharge of their shared responsibilities.

The Ephesian passage draws on the picture of the relationship of Christ and the church and so it would seem clear that, within the marriage relationship, there is a primary responsibility to serve placed upon the husband. However, in the passage in 1 Peter, note that, in the context of submission, wives are to mirror the attitudes of Christ and so reveal an aspect of Christ-likeness to their husbands. In fact both partners are to mirror aspects of Christ to one another.

When the exhortations to husbands and wives are laid side by side, the end result is that the husband also needs to be submissive. The fact that they are now one flesh speaks against any form of a domineering hierarchy, though the husband is given a responsibility to be the servant-leader by example within the marriage.

There is one other Scripture that is relevant here. In Colossians 3:18 Paul does not add the Greek phrase 'to your own husbands', but from the context it is clear that he is implying that this submission is to their own husbands. Paul simply says that wives are to submit to husbands.

So from the above we see that wives are asked to submit themselves to their own husbands. We also note that husbands are not told to subject their wives but that the submission must come from below. Further, the husband is told to love and care for his wife, as Christ loved the church, and to follow Christ in laying down his life for his wife.

The only Scripture where it could be argued that there is a submission of women to men in general would be 1 Corinthians 11:3—'the head of the woman is man'. This passage will be dealt with in more detail in a later section but we will make some initial comments specifically regarding the question being raised. There are different interpretations of 'head', but regardless of how we understand 'head ' let us note the following:

1. Paul does not use the word 'submit' within this passage. Consequently we should not see the passage commenting primarily on the issues of authority and submission.
2. Nor does he use the headship illustration as a basis to start an argument which has as its conclusion that all women need to be in submission to men. Rather he uses it as a basis for his argument of equality of function while retaining the gender distinction.
3. In the Greek Paul explicitly says of the male that 'the head of every male is Christ', but of the female he says 'the head of woman is the male'.[4] He does not repeat the word 'every' when he describes headship in relation to the woman. Whatever he means by 'head' he does not say that the male is the head of every female.
4. The Greek words translated as 'man' and 'woman' are interchangeable with the words for 'husband' and 'wife'—so there is some question as to which Paul means in these verses.
5. Because God is also said to be the head of Christ, we cannot argue for any lesser role or status being spoken of within these verses.

So we conclude that nowhere does the Scripture teach that all women are to be subject to all men, but it does teach explicitly that wives are to submit to their own husbands in the context of the marriage relationship. This does not mean that they can be rebellious elsewhere, but that they are to adopt the Christian response of submitting to one another in the fear of the Lord (Eph. 5:21). This last exhortation (submit to one another. . .)[5] is equally applicable to the husband, so he is not allowed to have an any less submissive attitude.

---

1. See Galations 5:20 where Paul refers to witchcraft as a 'work of the flesh' and not as a work of occult spirits.
2. Padgett, Alan, 'The Pauline rationale for submission', *Evangelical Quarterly*, Vol. LIX, No. 1, Jan. 1987. See

page 50 and conclusions on page 52.

3. Hull, Gretchen Gaebelein, *Equal to Serve*, (Scripture Union, 1989) page 205.

4. The NIV translation 'the head of the woman is man' makes a totally unnecessary change to the Greek, which places a definite article with 'man' and omits the article from 'woman'. Hence the strong argument for this phrase to be taken as a reference to the husband–wife relationship. The Greek reads as 'the head of a woman is the man'—that is, the man in relationship to her, her own husband.

5. The paragraph begins with verse 21, 'submit to one another . . .' and not with verse 22, 'wives submit to your husbands'. There is no verb 'submit' in verse 22, which is supplied from verse 21 where it does occur. So the primary exhortation placed on all believers is to adopt a submissive attitude in all their relationships out of fear of Christ.

CHAPTER 2

WOMAN AND WOMEN IN THE BIBLE

We are now going to look briefly at the subject of women in general and also at certain specific women within the Bible. This will not be an exhaustive study but will give us certain guidelines. These will be useful as we come to look at the specific passages of Scripture which have often been used to limit the role of women within the church. We will need to look at these passages in the light of the whole of Scripture. If we wrest verses away from their immediate context, or away from the overall teaching of Scripture, we will distort their truth. An example of the latter would be to say that the Bible teaches baptismal regeneration on the basis of 1 Peter 3:21 where we read, 'baptism ... now saves you'.

2.1 Genesis 1—3

We will begin by looking at the early chapters of Genesis. It is the book of 'beginnings' so we can expect to find there certain principles which will help us.

In Genesis 1 we see that both sexes are made in the image of God and that responsibility is laid on both their shoulders to fulfil God's commission. We could debate the meaning of the words 'image' and 'likeness' but for our purposes there seems to be no benefit in opening up that particular question. It is sufficient to say that both male and female bear the image of God—both are seen as equal in value, potential and destiny.

The commission is given equally to both of them and there is clearly no hint of subordination given within this chapter. We read this:

Then God said, 'Let us make man in our image,
in our likeness, and let them rule over the fish of
the sea and the birds of the air, over the live-
stock, over all the earth, and over all the creatures that move along the ground.'
So God created man
in his own image,
in the image of God
he created him;
male and female
he created them.
God blessed them and said to them, 'Be fruitful
and increase in number; fill the earth and sub-
due it. Rule over the fish of the sea and the birds
of the air and over every living creature that
moves on the ground' (Gen. 1:26–28).

In Genesis 2 we are introduced to Adam as male and to
his wife Eve. (In chapter 1 'Adam' is the word for hu-
mankind incorporating male and female; this is also the
case in Genesis 5:2.) This chapter (chapter 2) is often used
to teach that there was a clear subordination of the wife to
the husband; some even go further suggesting a subordination of all women to men.

There will certainly be general principles taught here
about the interrelationship of man and woman. Note,
however, that this passage portrays a specific relationship
of man and woman in terms of marriage—see verse 24,
'For this reason a man will leave his father and mother and
be united to his wife, and they will become one flesh'; and
again in Genesis 3:8 where we have 'the man and his wife'.
This indicates a distinction in relationships between men
and women according to their marital status. It is difficult
to see from the account in Genesis 1 any statement which
subordinates one gender to another. But even if we could
find such a statement, Genesis 2 only indicates its application in the context of marriage, never in a broad way
between the genders.

Woman is made from the man. This surely indicates the
relatedness of the two genders. She is not a separate

creation from the dust of the earth but is to be seen as 'bone of my bones and flesh of my flesh'. This certainly was Adam's response as indicated by his statement.

She is described as a suitable helper for Adam (Gen. 2:18). This should not be seen as implying that she is therefore inferior to the man but rather that she is his equal and in partnership with him. This word (Hebrew *ezer*) is used fifteen times of God in the Old Testament (out of a total of nineteen occurrences). It is not used to imply inferiority or subordination. It is rather teaching us that Adam and Eve were in partnership. There is a companionship between them (the man is no longer alone) and now the two together can complement each other as they fulfil their God-given commission.

There is an argument which draws on the rights of the first-born as described in certain Old Testament passages (e.g. Deut. 21:15–17). According to this, Adam (as first-born) is automatically in a position of authority, by nature of being created first. However, we can note that God overturned the rights of the first-born Himself in such examples as choosing Abel and Seth over Cain, Jacob over Esau and David over his brothers—so it is questionable how much weight can be given to this point.

Some have suggested that the fact that Adam named his wife shows a superiority of the man over the woman (Gen. 2:23). However, this verse does not contain the normal formula for naming, so again it is doubtful how much can be drawn from this.[1]

We can make a final note on verse 24, where it is clearly stated that it is the man who leaves the home of his parents to 'cleave' (KJV) to his wife. This word 'cleave' (Hebrew *dabaq*) is used almost universally of the weaker cleaving to the stronger, so for example it is used of Israel cleaving to God—Joshua 23:8; Psalm 91:14.[2] I am not suggesting that it is therefore teaching that the husband is to submit to his wife, but I am commenting on the fact that we need to bear this in mind if we are trying to read a 'creation order' into this passage.

If we look at this chapter and ask the question regarding a revealed order, we surely need to agree with Jewett when he says, 'So far as Genesis 2 is concerned, sexual hierarchy must be read into the text, it is not required by the text.'[3]

To speculate with regard to a fixed 'creation order' is at best purely academic. One can only assume that people lived in a harmony of relationship under the government of God before the entrance of sin into the world. In the same way we can say of a Christian marriage that the partners are to live and work together in harmony under the Lordship of Christ. The issue is not of one partner obeying the other but of both partners as one flesh submitting to and obeying the Lord. This is not to say that there is no leadership role resting on one partner, but it is emphasising that without a mutual submission to the Lord, there will be very little success in the relationship and plenty of opportunity for the conflict described in Genesis 3:16 to be manifested.

These first two chapters present the picture before sin entered the human race. Once sin arrived disruption was brought to the whole world and particularly to the area of relationships. It is no surprise to find that, from this point onwards, tension is present in all relationships, including marriage.

At this point we turn our attention to the third chapter of Genesis, which describes the entrance of sin and discord into the world of humanity. There are a number of points we need to consider, which I will list below.

1. There is no indication that woman is condemned for making a decision independent of man. I am not advocating independence as a virtue—but I am saying that we need to focus on the facts. Eve is wrong because of her action in submitting to Satan. To argue, as Pawson does in *Leadership is Male*,[4] that she took the masculine role, is surely to read something into the text which is certainly never explicitly stated.

2. To argue that Adam is the first to sin theologically because he allowed the woman to lead (i.e. a reversal of roles—as suggested by Pawson[5]) is not the result of a clear exegesis of this passage, but the result of an unwarranted

reading of a presupposition into the text. Genesis 3:6 suggests that Adam was present while the dialogue between Satan and Eve went on. It is possible that he is the first to sin because he simply stood by without speaking up—i.e. he was culpable because he was passive. This would have been equally true of the woman had she stood there observing the situation and allowed the man to eat of the forbidden fruit without speaking up for the truth. (Jas. 4:17—'Anyone, then, who knows the good he ought to do and doesn't do it, sins.')

3. In taking this argument of role reversal further we would need to ask some questions. What was the feminine role before the Fall? We know that Adam and Eve were to live in partnership—they were both created in the image of God and they were both commissioned with regard to the earth. One can only assume that they flowed in harmony together before the entrance of sin and that the question of leadership was, at most, purely academic.

4. To say that Adam's mistake was that he put himself in the feminine role in following his wife is surely not the issue. The problem was that he followed her in disobedience. It would be equally true that, if the woman follows the man and therefore enters into sin, she is to be blamed. We need only to look at the case of Ananias and Sapphira in the New Testament to see this. She is equally judged alongside her husband—she could not plead in her defence that she was simply fulfilling the feminine role! [6]

5. Eve did not use deception as an excuse—rather she explained the reality. Adam, however, blamed Eve, and ultimately God, for the problem. He refused to take responsibility for the situation. So to argue he is more fit to lead than Eve (as some would from Paul's statements regarding Eve's deception in 1 Timothy 2:11–15) is rather strange. [7]

6. Again we must be careful not to read into the text with regard to why Satan approached Eve and not Adam.

I suggest the text does not bear out any teaching that Satan approached Eve because women are more easily deceived. I have even seen it suggested (albeit tongue in cheek) that Satan approached Eve because he knew she was the 'bottom line' and so Adam would naturally follow![8] I say this by way of warning—we must let the text speak for itself. We are simply not told why Satan first approached Eve and not Adam.

7. They are both punished—God treats both as responsible beings. The wife is not judged as a servant of the husband but as an individual in her own right.

8. The result of sin was a break in relationship between God and man—and also damage to the relationship between husband and wife.

9. The effect of this discord is described in Genesis 3:16. From now on, the sexes are, to some extent, at war. It is difficult to ascertain the correct meaning of the phrase, 'Your desire (Hebrew *tesucah*) will be for your husband,' but it would appear that it has a direct parallel in the Hebrew of Genesis 4:7, where sin is seen to have a desire to control Cain.[9] So the result is a tension: the woman will desire to rule her husband, but, in the end, the husband will tend to dominate the woman. This would seem to be the situation which Peter addresses in 1 Peter 3:7, 'Husbands . . . treat them with respect as the weaker partner'.

2.1.1 Conclusions from Genesis 1—3

It would seem that there is no evidence from these passages to suggest that there is a distinct or inherent order in male/female relationships before the entrance of sin. Subsequent to the Fall there is tension in all relationships and specifically in those between the sexes. This battle of the sexes is recorded throughout the remainder of Scripture and of history.

2.2 Introduction to post-Eden Scripture

It is important to remember that Scripture makes an accurate record of history, but that does not mean God automatically endorses what is recorded. Humanity is fallen and the redemption of fallen humanity is not complete (in the sense of the price being paid) until Christ comes as the fulfilment of the promise in Genesis 3:15. Even after His coming we are to outwork the great redemption that He has purchased.

The Old Covenant is but a shadow of the New. So when we study the Old Testament Scriptures we must bear this in mind. The Gospels themselves deal with a period prior to the coming of the New Covenant, so cannot be used as the final statement on the New Covenant. The Old Testament record and the Gospels are important: but the teaching that we find in the remainder of the New Testament is where we must base our pattern for the role and ministry of women.

The remainder of the New Testament records both doctrine and practice. Practice usually comes out of doctrine and so a discovery of New Testament practice is important to us. However, there were times when there was an apparent compromise of doctrine for a specific purpose. One clear example of this is when Paul circumcised Timothy (Acts 16:3). I say this so that we are clear that there could be, at times, a conflict over what was put into practice and what was taught as doctrine. Where there is a conflict, the specific teaching of Scripture must take primacy over the record of early church practice.

2.2.1 Roles of women in the Old Testament

We could summarise the Old Testament picture as saying that woman tended to have an inferior role in the religious and social domain, though this did not prevent her from fulfilling on occasions the highest functions within the nation (e.g. military leader or prophetess). However, the general picture is of her place being in the home.

For our purposes we note Miriam, Deborah and Huldah. Miriam was a prophetess who was involved in leadership alongside Aaron and Moses. Micah 6:4 says, 'I sent Moses to lead you, also Aaron and Miriam.'

Deborah was a woman who clearly exercised leadership in the political, military, civil and religious spheres (Judg. 4). If the other judges were leaders (and they certainly were) then there is no reason to say that she was not a significant leader of Israel at this time.

Huldah exercised prophetic ministry and was a contemporary of Jeremiah and Zephaniah (so the argument of God using a woman because He could not find a man is certainly not applicable here). Five national male leaders came to her for advice as to the instructions of the Lord concerning the book of the law which Josiah had found (2 Chron. 34:14–28).

2.2.2 The woman of Proverbs 31
Proverbs 31:10–31 presents a picture of the 'ideal' woman. Here we have a woman who was anything but the image of a demure female sitting at home doing the washing up and darning her husband's socks! Far from it — she was a, or perhaps even *the,* major contributor to the welfare and upkeep of her family.

It is interesting to note the Septuagint translation here. (The Septuagint was a Greek translation of the Hebrew Scriptures and is often quoted from in the New Testament. From this point on we will refer to it by its normal abbreviation—LXX.) The LXX translates the Hebrew of verse 10 (fairly accurately but boldly) as 'A manly woman who can find?'! Compare this with the NIV—'A wife of noble character who can find?'

2.2.3 The role of women in first-century Judaism and beyond.
There is no question that women were now assigned a very inferior status. They were only taught the domestic arts; they were considered unfit to learn anything beyond that. When the people came to the synagogue, the men came to learn and the women to listen (contrast this with Paul in 1 Timothy 2:11 where his Greek reads 'let a woman learn . . . '.)

There are many quotes we could give but perhaps the prayer of the Jewish male will summarise the situation: 'Praise be to God, he has not created me a Gentile; praise be to God that he has not created me a woman; praise be to God that he has not created me an ignorant man.' [10]

The situation in the Roman world was not dissimilar—women were generally seen as inferior to men.

Alongside this we need to note that there were a number of wealthy and influential women involved in Christianity. This could be the reason for the requirement that women do not adorn themselves outwardly (as in 1 Timothy 2:9,10). If this was the situation referred to in this passage, then it could point to these capable women coming into the assembled body and lording it over others (possibly including their husbands). So Paul would be saying—let them learn but with the right attitude (see 1 Timothy 2:9–15).

2.2.4 Key women in the New Testament

For the sake of brevity I will not look at the situation in the Gospels—suffice it to say that Jesus treated women with a respect which they had seldom before experienced. He taught them and used them as examples in His parables. There were women who followed Him and we know that Mary sat at His feet—which was a technical term for being a disciple (Luke 8:1–3; 10:39).[11] Some of His longest and most significant recorded conversations were with women. An example of this is found in John 4:7–30 and His conversation with the woman from Samaria. It is clear that He continually gave women back their dignity.

The first people to whom Jesus revealed Himself after the resurrection were women. This is highly significant because the Jewish society of that time would not allow the testimony of a woman to stand in court.[12] However, Jesus was prepared to entrust Himself to them as the first bearers of the resurrection Gospel. To read into this the priority of women over men in the post-resurrection era is perhaps to read too much into these narratives; but it clearly underlines how Jesus came to restore women to a place of trust equal to men. We will address the issue of

Jesus choosing twelve men as His apostles at a later stage.

In the New Testament there are clearly a number of women who were involved in ministry and leadership. I will list a number of these below, starting with some who are mentioned in Romans 16.

1. Phoebe is called a deacon of the church in Cenchrea (Romans 16:1). This is clearly an office of leadership—I suggest it is an office of government, where the deacons served the oversight.[13] In line with this it seems best to take the reference in 1 Timothy 3:11 to refer to women serving as deacons as opposed to deacons' wives.

Incidentally, the reference (in 1 Timothy 3:12) to deacons being the husband of but one wife might help us to realise that the similar statement with regard to elders (in 1 Timothy 3:1) does not necessarily by itself exclude women from being elders, any more than it excludes single men or widowers.

So we could say that Paul expected elders to be male with children but did not insist that they had to be male, married and fathers—otherwise Paul himself and even Jesus would have been excluded! So we can see that he is assuming they will be male but not excluding the possibility of female ones.

Phoebe had been a great help to Paul. (The Greek word here is *prostatis* : protectress, patroness, a woman set over others. This is related to the word for leadership: *proistamenos*.) This word by itself would not necessarily mean that she was therefore a leader, but it is interesting to note the use of the same root word. When it is placed alongside the word 'deacon' we get the picture of an influential woman in some form of leadership role.

2. Priscilla (and Aquila). They achieve equal standing together and were a well-developed husband–wife ministry team. There are six references to them in the New Testament and in four of them Priscilla is named first. We do not know the significance of this—perhaps she was from a higher social background, or perhaps she was the more active member in the ministry.[14]

3. (Andronicus) and Junia (Rom. 16:7). There is overwhelming evidence that the second name here is feminine and it seems likely that they are a husband–wife team. They are said to be outstanding among the apostles— Cranfield says that the way this Greek phrase was understood by all the known patristic writers is that they were themselves apostles.[15] (Incidentally all the patristic authors also took Junia to be feminine.[16]) So here we have a woman exercising authority as an apostle, probably alongside her husband.

4. Tryphena, Tryphosa, Persis and Mary (Rom. 16:6,12) are all described as having worked hard. What this entailed we do not know but it would seem to mean that these were people who moved in ministry. In 1 Corinthians 16:16 the Corinthian Christians are exhorted to submit to those who are involved in the work and who labour at it.

5. Nympha led, or at least hosted, a house church (Col. 4:15). The church usually met in the home, so this is more than a house-group. It seems reasonable to assume that Nympha had some sort of leadership role within this church.

6. Syntyche and Euodia were fellow workers with Paul (Phil. 4:2,3). They worked alongside him for the sake of the Gospel and would appear to have been on equal terms with his other fellow workers, many of whom were male.

7. The 'elect' (KJV) lady of 2 John. Opinion is divided as to what this term means. However, we do know from later church history that 'elect person' was used of someone who held office within the church. So it is possible that this refers to a female leader in this church.

2.2.5 Conclusions

There seems to be very strong evidence to see women exercising every gift and ministry within the New Testament. There is also strong evidence that many worked with Paul on equal terms with the men, and that there was at least one woman who was specifically called an apostle. (Although a very weak argument could be advanced that she could only fulfil this because she was married.)

We are still left with the question—were there any women elders? There is no direct evidence on this from within the New Testament, nor would there appear to be any direct prohibition of women fulfilling this role. 1 Timothy 3:1 uses the generic term, 'If anyone sets his heart on being an overseer' and, as we have seen above, it is highly unlikely Paul is excluding single men, or those without children, through giving this list of qualifications. So it is also unlikely that he was excluding women, although his expectation at this time was that they would probably be male.

From the New Testament it would appear that women have a greater role in the churches in Macedonia and Rome than in Jerusalem and the more Eastern regions—probably reflecting the different degrees of cultural freedom offered women in different areas.

2.3 Equality through the Gospel—an equality to serve

Gretchen Gaebelein Hull in her book *Equal to Serve* says, 'Secular feminism centres around gaining equal rights; biblical feminism centres around equal opportunity to serve.'[17] This is the issue at stake. We are not looking at who can rule (a worldly model of leadership) but who can have authority to serve.

Under the New Covenant it is not the outward shell that is important but the life within. Paul says the outward shell is wasting away (2 Cor. 4:16) but the life within is eternal (v. 18). It is the life source within which is important—the promised Holy Spirit who is poured out on all flesh, irrespective of gender. Because of this we no longer consider people from a worldly point of view but as new creatures in Christ (2 Cor. 5:16,17). This outward shell must extend to cover the issue of gender. To see people restricted because of their gender is surely to take a worldly viewpoint.

God offers the same renewal and salvation to all—regardless of race, gender or class. He also gives the same high calling, responsibility and privilege to all. Both male and female are equal ambassadors for Christ and His Gospel (2 Cor. 5:14–21).

Finally we come to the verse of Scripture which must be considered if we want to do justice to the liberation of the Gospel—'There is neither Jew nor Greek, slave nor free, male nor female, for you are all one in Christ Jesus' (Gal. 3:28). All barriers go down as a result of the unity we find ourselves in with regard to our inheritance in Christ. This inheritance covers our redemption, commission, purpose and usefulness. It does away with the divisions of race, class and gender.

As a result of the Fall men and women became adversaries, competitors and even oppressors—instead of co-operators and joint administrators of our inheritance. In Christ this harmony is restored to us. Male and female can again jointly administrate the original commission God gave of bringing His rule to bear on the earth. We are qualified to do so because both male and female are being transformed into His image (2 Cor. 3:18 cf. Gen. 1:26–28).

The Gospel message of liberation is a fitting close for this chapter. There are many different perspectives regarding the role of women, but on one point there is surely total agreement—the Gospel comes to liberate. It comes to make us into the men and women God wants us to be.

---

1. Evans, Mary, *Woman in the Bible* (Paternoster Press, 1983) page 16, point c.
2. Ibid., page 17.
3. Jewett, P.K., *Man as Male and Female* (Eerdmans, 1975) page 126.
4. Pawson, David, *Leadership is Male* (Highland Books, 1988) page 23.
5. Ibid., pages 22–25.
6. Acts 5:1–11.
7. Pawson, op. cit., page 23.
8. Mickelsen, Alvera, 'Does order of creation, redemption, and

climax demand female supremacy?', essay as appendix in Hull, op. cit., pages 245–250.

9. Evans, op. cit., pages 19, 20.
10. Tosephta Barakhoth, 7, 8, quoted in Trombley, Charles, *Who Said Women Can't Teach?* (Logos, 1985) page 29.
11. Cf. Acts 22:3 where Paul says he had studied at the feet of Gamaliel.
12. Josephus, *The Antiquities of the Jews*, Book IV, viii. 15.
13. Paul uses a masculine noun 'deacon' and not the feminine verbal participle. If he used the latter it could indicate simply that she was a servant, but by using the masculine noun it would seem to indicate that she held office in the church at Cenchrea.
14. Trombley, op. cit. page 194, quotes John Chrystostom's comments on the change of the order with Priscilla's name coming first. Chrystostom says, 'He did not do so without reason: the wife must have had, I think, greater piety than her husband. This is not simple conjecture; its confirmation is evident in the Acts.'
15. Cranfield, *Romans 2* (T & T Clark, 1975; ICC Commentary series).
16. Clark, Andrew, 'Apostleship', in *Vox Angelica*, Vol. XIX, 1989.
17. Hull, op. cit., page 56.

PART TWO

INTRODUCTION

In Part One of this study we opened up the subject of men, women, and their interrelationship and how this is expressed in the context of the church. A brief framework was outlined which culminated in the appeal to see everything through the message of the liberating Gospel. All theology needs to be Christo-centric; and in Christ there is full and equal redemption for all people regardless of race, gender or social background.

In Part Two, we plan to delve a little deeper into two distinct and important areas. Firstly we'll take a look at the meaning of the Greek word *kephale* (translated as 'head'), and, secondly, at the specific passages in the New Testament that have traditionally been used to limit the role of women within the church. Finally there is a brief response to a number of questions which are often raised regarding the role of women.

I do not ask that you agree with all of my conclusions, nor do I profess to have answered all the questions which can and should be asked. However, I do believe it is necessary for us to consider the issue seriously. There are many women asking the legitimate question of how they can effectively serve the One who came to set them free.

CHAPTER 3

THE MEANING OF *KEPHALE*

The first part of this study on the meaning of *kephale* in Greek literature is of a fairly technical nature. Much of the material presented here is owed to the work of Turner and Cotterell in their book *Linguistics and Biblical Interpretation* (SPCK, 1989). I suggest that if anyone would like to follow this through in a fuller way, they read pages 141–145 and 316–328 of that book.

For those who do not want to get involved in the technicalities of the meaning of the word *kephale* in Greek literature, I suggest that you pick up this chapter at 3.2, where the metaphorical uses of *kephale* in the New Testament are considered.

3.1 What does *kephale* mean in Greek literature?

The Greek word *kephale* is translated by the English word 'head'. As in English, the normal use of this word is simply anatomical. Paul also used the word metaphorically and it is over this use of the word that we will now need to make some decisions. There are two alternatives which we can explain as follows—*kephale* is either 'head' as in the head of a department (i.e. one who directs and has authority) or it is 'head' as in the source of a river (so carrying no connotation of authority).

Arguments have been put forward on both sides. For instance, A. and B. Michelson's article in *Christianity Today* [1] argues for the meaning of 'source'. In fact they go so far as to say, 'Superior rank...does not appear in secular Greek of New Testament times.' This can be contrasted with David M. Park, who puts forward evidence of 'head' being used of those presiding in authority.[2] Perhaps, to date, the paper by Catherine Kroeger, which was delivered to the Evangelical Theological Society in 1986, is one of the best argued and documented papers on *kephale* as 'source'. She also includes material from the Church Fathers which covers their interpretation of Paul's words in 1 Corinthians 11 'the head of the woman is man'.[3]

The above three articles can serve as examples of some of the recent writings on the meaning of *kephale*. We now need to examine some of the arguments being advanced which push us in the direction of 'head' meaning 'source'. I do not want to oversimplify the issue but we can look at some of them under the points as listed below.

1. The LXX uses both *kephale* and *arche* (beginning) to translate the Hebrew word *rosh* (head). So it is argued that *kephale* was synonymous with *arche* (thus *kephale* means 'beginning' or 'source').[4]

However, when the various references are considered, it would appear to be the case that *kephale* is never used to translate *rosh* when the latter meant 'beginning' (as in time sequence). So, this would point us away from believing that the translators of the LXX saw *kephale* as carrying a metaphorical meaning of 'beginning'.

There is one occurrence when *rosh* might mean 'source' (Gen. 2:10). Again, it is interesting that the translators did not use the word *kephale* but rather the word *arche* at this point. So again it would appear that the translators did not accept that 'source' was one possible meaning of *kephale*. Whenever *rosh* might have carried the meaning of 'beginning' or 'source' it seems that the translators were careful that they did not at that point use the Greek word *kephale*—surely this is because they knew that *kephale* could not carry those meanings.

So the argument from the LXX translation would actually seem to point us in the opposite direction from those who have quoted it to advance the suggestion that *kephale* normally meant 'source' when used in a metaphorical way.

Following on from this there are clear references in the LXX to *kephale* meaning 'person in authority'. In the story of Jephthah (Judg. 10 and 11) we read that the man who will begin to fight against the sons of Ammon . . . will become head (*archon* in some MSS but *kephale* in others) over all the inhabitants of Gilead (Judg. 10:18). Subsequently, Jephthah is selected by the elders as the man who would be the Israelites' head (*kephale*) and captain (*archegos*) (Judg. 11:11).

There is the further reference in 2 Samuel 22:44 where David declares 'you have delivered me from the attacks of my people; you have preserved me as the head (*kephale*) of nations' (LXX).

So it would appear that the translators used the word *kephale* in a metaphorical way to refer to a person in authority and never with the sense of source.

2. Another argument is that *kephale* was used of the source of a river.[5] Alongside this, though, we need to lay out the fact that *kephale* is also used of the mouth of a river.[6] The easiest explanation would be that *kephale* is being applied to the source or mouth of a river in the sense of 'extreme end'—both the source and the mouth are the extreme end so either can be called the *kephale* of the river. 'Extreme end' is a meaning which is well established (for example, it would appear that both ends of the poles used to carry the ark of the covenant are called 'heads' in this sense).[7] So there is no need to posit a new meaning here for which we would have no corroborating evidence. One extreme end (head) of a river is its source; the other extreme end is its mouth.

So it is true to say that the source of a river is called the *kephale* of the river but this does not mean of itself that 'head' and 'source' carry equivalent meanings—in fact because 'head' can refer to both ends of a river it points us away from the claim that 'head' and 'source' are equivalent.

Further, even if there were sufficient evidence to suggest that an accepted and established meaning of the word *kephale* was '(river) source', this would not then mean that *kephale* would have a general meaning of 'source' when used metaphorically. As Cotterell and Turner say,

'And where have we evidence of this? Where do we find instances of such statements as "cows are the *kephale* of milk"; "Egypt is the *kephale* of papyrus", etc.'[8] There is, however, no such evidence of this type available to us. So we conclude that there is no evidence of *kephale* being used universally to mean 'source'.

3. The head of a deity as source. This is taken from the Orphic fragments 21a, 'Zeus was first, Zeus is last ... Zeus the head, Zeus the middle . . .' Some manuscripts have 'head' here, others have a variant reading and use the word 'beginning'—*arche*. So, it is claimed, this points us in the direction of accepting that *arche* and *kephale* are interchangeable and that they both mean 'source'. However, we need to remember that *arche*, like *kephale*, can mean 'beginning' without meaning 'source'—and this meaning is probably the best suited to this context. Again Cotterell and Turner lay out a good guiding principle on this when they say, 'As we are able to explain *kephale* along a well-established sense of the word, it is barely legitimate to use the fragment as evidence of an otherwise unattested sense "source".' [9]

4. The head was seen to be the source of a variety of substances pertinent to life. For example, Artemidorus maintains, 'The head is the source of light and life for the body'.[10] However, we need to ask—how would this draw us to the conclusion that 'head' actually means 'source'? Cotterell and Turner use the following examples to clarify the confusion which using this sort of evidence brings: employers are the source of our income and books are the source of our knowledge. However, this does not mean that the words 'employer' and 'book' can now be used metaphorically to mean 'source'.[11]

Wayne Grudem has shown that the sense 'ruler', 'chief', 'authority over', etc. for the word *kephale* is not unknown amongst the nonliteral uses of the word.[12] It is certainly an established meaning in the Greek Septuagint. Grudem also examined an extensive number of examples of the use of the word *kephale* and concluded that the pre-Christian literature showed no occasion at all when *kephale* unambiguously meant 'source' or 'origin', and those very few contexts which had previously been appealed to failed to substantiate such a sense.

Conclusion with regard to the meaning of kephale in Greek literature

There is considerable evidence of 'head' being used in the sense of 'ruler' in pre-Christian literature, while there is no unambiguous evidence of 'head' being used to mean 'source' before the third century AD. Cotterell and Turner conclude that 'such evidence may of course turn up; but until it does it remains linguistically less than responsible to say "source" was one of the (pre-Christian) senses of the word *kephale*'. [13]

It seems that the only conclusion we can make is to say that 'source' or 'origin' was not a conventional sense of the word *kephale* in Paul's time and there would not appear to be any external evidence to suggest that Paul was now introducing a new meaning into the word *kephale*.

This then leaves us to look at the passages where Paul uses the word *kephale* metaphorically.

3.2 Passages where *kephale* is used metaphorically

There are seven New Testament passages where 'head' is used in a metaphorical sense. We will now look at these in turn, beginning with those where there might seem to be a possibility of 'head' taking on the meaning of 'source'.

3.2.1 Colossians 2:19

'He has lost connection with the Head, from whom the whole body, supported and held together by its ligaments and sinews, grows as God causes it to grow.'

Clearly, Christ is seen as the source of nourishment for the church in this passage. However, when we examine the Greek Paul uses in this verse, I believe we shall see he never accepted that the word 'head' actually meant 'source'.

The word *kephale* is a feminine noun in Greek but the relative pronoun (from whom) is in the masculine. If the pronoun were to refer back to the word 'head' it would have to be in the feminine gender. So it is not accurate to say that the body grows from the head—implying a meaning of 'source' or 'origin'. It grows from the one who is the head of the body. The one who nourishes the body is obviously Christ, who is also the head of the body. With regard to the meaning of *kephale*, it would seem that Paul avoided using the feminine relative pronoun for the simple reason that he knew that 'head' (*kephale*) did not mean 'source'.

3.2.2 Ephesians 4:15–16

'... grow up into him who is the Head, that is Christ. From him the whole body, joined and held together by every supporting ligament, grows and builds itself up in love, as each part does its work.'

The same comments as above apply with regard to the Greek of this verse. The relative pronoun is masculine here, so referring to Christ (from Him). It is not feminine, which would make it refer to 'head' (from which the whole body grows—so causing 'head' to mean 'source').

3.2.3 Colossians 1:17–18

'He is before all things, and in him all things hold together. And he is the head of the body, the church; he is the beginning and the firstborn from among the dead, so that in everything he might have the supremacy.'

Paul is expressing the total supremacy of Christ in this section of his letter to Colossae. This supremacy was being challenged by the Colossian heresy, so it would seem natural to take 'head' here to mean that the church is subject to Christ (as is the whole universe). The term 'head' asserts His inseparability from the body but it also excludes His identity with it.

3.2.4 Ephesians 1:20–23

' . . . appointed him to be head over everything for the church . . .'

Here Paul is showing Christ has an exalted position over all things. It is clearly a position of authority and Paul explicitly uses the Greek preposition *huper* which means 'over and above', 'beyond', 'more than'. There would seem to be no hint in these verses that Paul thought 'head' implied any sense of the word 'source'.

3.2.5 Colossians 2:10
'... You have been given fullness in Christ, who is the Head over every power and authority.'

Here we again conclude that 'head' is carrying the concept of 'supremacy'. It is possible to say that Christ is the source of every power and authority but the overall context of this passage is of the supremacy of Christ. He is the exalted one and has no rivals. In this sense He is the head of all things—including every power and authority. This is already His position by nature of His work. Paul states that the fulfilment of all this will take place when all things in heaven and earth are put back into proper order under that one head, Christ (Eph. 1:10 where he uses the word *anakephalaioo*).

Conclusion drawn from the above passages
When we take these passages together, we may conclude that 'head' is being used to mean the superiority of Christ over the church and all creation, including all powers and authorities. It would seem most likely that Paul used the same word consistently throughout these two similar letters.

I am therefore concluding at this stage that Paul understood that 'head' did not mean 'source'. This seems most clear where he attributes the source of the growth of the church to Christ, but carefully avoids saying that the head is the source of this growth.

We will therefore expect the same meaning to be carried through to the final passages which deal with the marriage relationship (and possibly also the relationship of men and women).

3.2.6 Ephesians. 5:22–33
'Submit to one another out of reverence for Christ. Wives,

(submit) to your husbands as to the Lord. For the husband is the head of the wife as also Christ is the head of the church, his body, of which he is the Saviour. Now as the church submits to Christ, so also wives should submit to their husbands in everything . . .'

I have put the word 'submit' in brackets because it is not included in verse 23—from the Greek construction it is understood that it needs to be supplied from verse 22. For this reason we need to see verse 22 as the start of this passage. Mutual submission is a requirement of all believers. Husbands, too, need to submit, as we are all living our lives out on the basis that we have to give an account to Christ Himself.

Paul then gives the reason why wives need to submit to their husbands. He uses the word *hoti*—'because', 'for'. Mutual submission is required but that does not negate an order within the marriage relationship. Wives are explicitly told to submit because of this order. Order does not necessarily imply superiority but does imply a greater responsibility—this is surely the case here as Paul goes on to describe the sacrificial love which the husband is to have for his wife. He is to lay his life down for her and serve her, even as Christ has done for the church.

At the beginning of verse 24, where the NIV has the word 'Now', Paul actually uses the word *alla*—'but'. Some have taken this to mean that Paul is stressing that, although the husband is the servant of his wife (i.e. 'head' as 'source') he quickly covers himself by saying in effect that this does not mean that the wife can lord it over her husband. [14]

However, this is very unlikely—Paul has already stated that the reason the wife is to submit to her husband is 'because (*hoti*) the husband is the head of the wife'. There are other possible explanations for the use of the word *alla* which would fit the context well. The headship of Christ is so much superior to the headship of the husband (Paul has just stated that Christ is the Saviour of his body), that he puts in this strong negative word, stating in effect 'but in spite of this great difference' submission is still required. The other possible reason concerns the 'resumptive use' of this word *alla*. The 'resumptive use' was used to fix attention on the special point of immediate interest. If this is the situation here then it would mean in effect that Paul is saying 'but I am talking about the husband–wife relationship'.

We conclude that the use of 'head' here is to show us that Paul believed in an order within the marriage relationship. There is no superiority but the husband carries the greater responsibility within the relationship. This responsibility is outlined in the verses which follow. The wife, too, has great responsibility and we must never lose sight of the fact that they are both to submit to the Lord as one flesh, as well as to one another in the fear of Christ.

3.2.7 1 Corinthians 11:3

'Now I want you to realise that the head of every man is Christ, and the head of the woman is man, and the head of Christ is God.' (This is the NIV version, but see point 4 below.)

I will comment in greater detail on this passage in the next chapter, when we look at specific passages of Scripture which relate to women. However, we need to look at the issue of 'head' at this point.

If 'head' were to mean 'source' here, we would need to ask in what way can it be said that God is the source of Christ? Indeed in what way can man be the source of woman—other than in the historic sense of Eve being created from Adam? On the issue of God being the head of Christ, we do know that within this same letter (15:24–28) Paul clearly taught some form of submission of the Son to the Father. Again we need to remember that this does not mean that Christ is inferior. So headship is not a reference to inferiority but is a description of order within relationships.

Another question which this passage raises concerns the meaning of the words 'woman' and 'man'. The Greek words translated 'man' and 'woman' are the same as the Greek words for 'husband' and 'wife'. There is a divergence of opinion as to the meaning in these verses. Cotterell and Turner say, 'We would not necessarily be wrong in understanding the passage as dealing with husbands and wives, but it must be admitted that there are no strong grounds within the text for restricting the subject in this way'.[15]

However, I suggest that it is in fact referring to husbands and wives for the following reasons:

1. In another passage in this same letter dealing with order in worship, Paul specifically deals with husbands and wives (1 Cor. 14 :34–36).

2. In Ephesians 5:23 he has already stated that the husband is the head of the wife and he consistently requires wives to submit to their own husbands—whereas there are no specific commands for all women to submit to all men (see 1.4—Do all women need to submit to men?). If this is being introduced here, then it is an entirely new concept which is unsupported elsewhere in Scripture. I would suggest that the Ephesian passage gives us a precedent in terms of our understanding here.

3. He does not use this statement to limit the women in terms of their function. Nor does he argue for their submission to all men who are present, which we could expect if he were arguing for a clear subordination of all women to all men. Further, as his argument develops, it would seem to be, 'most convincingly presented as it affected the relationship between husbands and wives. It does not appear reasonable to suppose that if a woman prayed with her head not covered she dishonoured all the men in the church'. [16]

4. The Greek which he uses, I believe, points us towards a translation of the words as 'husband' and 'wife'. Paul begins by saying that the head of every male (or husband) is Christ but he does not go on to say (as one might expect) that the head of every woman is the male. In the Greek he limits it to the head of 'a woman' is 'the man' (notice how this differs from the NIV translation). The definite article which goes with 'man' (the man) defines who is the head of woman—it is not every male figure but the man, i.e. her own husband. J. Armitage Robinson in fact translates this

as 'a woman's head is her husband'. [17]

E. Earle Ellis translates this as 'the head of every husband is Christ, the head of the wife is the husband, and the head of Christ is God. . . the husband (exists as) the image and glory of God, but the wife is the glory of the husband' (1 Cor. 11:3,7). [18] So by taking it to be husband and wife we are able to keep the teaching in this passage within the harmony of the other Scriptures on this subject.

Conclusion on the meaning of kephale

My conclusion, having examined both the Greek literature of the day and the passages of Scripture where 'head' is used metaphorically, is that it would appear that 'head' does not, in fact, mean 'source' within the New Testament. It would seem to be the case that it carried with it the clear meaning of a person who has been endowed with authority in the particular situation which is being described.

In all our discussions we need to keep coming back to the starting point of this book—the nature of Kingdom authority. To be appointed as head does not mean that one has authority to domineer—rather it gives that person a greater responsibility to serve.

At this point I believe we are ready to go on to look at the specific passages of Scripture which have been used to limit the role of women in the body of Christ.

---

1. *Christianity Today*, 20 Feb. 1981.
2. *Evangelical Quarterly*, April 1987.
3. This paper appears as Appendix 3 in Hull, op. cit., pages 267–283.
4. 'The meaning of *kephale* in the Pauline epistles', *Journal of Theological Studies*, Vol. 5, 1954.
5. Herodotus 4.91 (the source of the Tearus).
6. Callmachus, *Aetia* 2.46.
7. 3 Kings 8:8 LXX.
8. Cotterell and Turner, *Linguistics and Biblical Interpretation* (SPCK, 1989) page 143.
9. Ibid., page 143.
10. Daldiensis, Artemidorus, *Oneirocritica*, 2.7, as quoted by Kroeger in Appendix 3 of Hull, op. cit., page 271.

11. Cotterell and Turner, op. cit., page 144.
12. 'Does *kephale* mean "source" or "authority over" in Greek literature? A survey of 2336 examples', *Trinity Journal*, Vol. 6, 1985.
13. Cotterell and Turner, op. cit., page 144.
14. Evans, op. cit., page 75.
15. Cotterell and Turner, op. cit., page 318.
16. Cotterell and Turner, op. cit., page 322.
17. Robinson, J. Armitage, *St Paul's Epistle to the Ephesians* (Macmillan & Co, 1903) page 205.
18. Ellis, E. Earle, *Pauline Theology—Ministry and Society* (Eerdmans/Paternoster, 1989) pages 59–60.

CHAPTER 4

SPECIFIC PASSAGES OF SCRIPTURE RELATING TO WOMEN

We will deal with a passage of Scripture in 1 Peter which has been misused to teach the absolute obedience of a wife to her husband—this would go right against all we laid out on authority and submission in chapter 1 so it is important that we clarify this Scripture first. We will then look at the three so-called 'difficult passages' in 1 Corinthians and 1 Timothy.

4.1 1 Peter 3:1–7—Women to obey their hus– bands

This passage of Scripture has been taken to mean that the wife owes absolute obedience to her husband. So, it has been taught, a woman is to obey her husband with an absolute obedience, even if that places the wife in a posi- tion where she ends up doing something which would clearly go against the teaching of Scripture. The argument runs that the wife is accountable to her husband and is to obey him in all things, while he is accountable to God.

We have already stated that only God can command absolute obedience from us (see the comments under the earlier discussion on authority and submission), but we now need to look more closely at this passage to see exactly what is being taught here.

Firstly, I believe it has a wider application than just to women whose husbands are unsaved, as some have sug- gested, so making the command here to be purely pragmatic in order to win the unsaved husbands. Peter's words 'if any of them do not believe the word' does not restrict the injunction ('wives . . . be submissive to your husbands') solely to marriages where the husband is unsaved, but it certainly includes those marriages.

So he is telling all wives to submit to their own husbands (he uses the explicit Greek phrase *tois idiois andrasin*: 'to your own husbands') and then uses the Old Testament example of women submitting to their husbands and the example of Sarah in particular.

Like Paul he does not simply place a requirement on the wife, but places clear obligations also on the husband. These obligations are found in verse 7. The husband is to live with his wife and show her consideration and respect. As far as their inheritance in God is concerned they are absolutely equal, but as far as their relationship is concerned the wife is described as the weaker partner (lit. 'weaker vessel'). Peter does not explain what he means by this phrase, but it could certainly be interpreted that the husband is at an advantage in the relationship (from a human point of view). It is because of this advantage (i.e. he could lord it over his wife) that he is explicitly instructed to live with his wife in a considerate and respectful way. If he does exploit his advantage in the relationship that would be an abuse of authority and would result in his prayers being hindered.

The story of Abraham and Sarah has been taken by some to back up their argument that women are to obey their husbands in all things, even if that were to lead them into sin themselves. I believe this is reading too much into the story and does not deal adequately with the second half of verse 6.

The end of verse 5 and the beginning of verse 6 teaches that women are to respect their husbands and be submissive in heart. However, the second half of verse 6 teaches that women are not daughters of Sarah if they simply do whatever they are told, regardless of the morality of that command. Quite the contrary—they are only daughters of Sarah if they do what is right and do not back down through fear (even if that means they have to hold through in the face of their own husbands). This then fits in with our original premise that only God can command absolute obedience.

One example from the story of Abraham and Sarah will suffice on this point. In Genesis 21:8–13 we find that Sarah tells Abraham to send Ishmael away. God eventually intervenes in the situation and instructs Abraham to 'listen to whatever Sarah tells you'. In other words Sarah had heard from God and as she held through, Abraham was in fact instructed by God to submit to her in this situation. So the obedience required from women in 1 Peter 3 cannot be absolute—nor would we expect it to be so in the light of our earlier studies. Absolute obedience can only be given to God and His word. Abraham has to obey Sarah here because she brought the word of God into the situation.

Any obedience within human relationships can only be conditional—absolute obedience is to be given to God alone. Husbands and wives are to live together in harmony and they are both to submit to the Living God. This individual submission to God will mean that a wife is to hold through, in every situation, with what is righteous and godly. By so doing she will be a daughter of Sarah because she has not given way to fear.

One other example from the New Testament might help. We know from Acts chapter 5 that Ananias and Sapphira are both equally judged for their decision to lie to the apostles. Sapphira could not hide behind her husband and say that she was simply submitting to him and being obedient. They were both accountable to God and had to answer to Him individually for their actions.

We conclude that this passage in 1 Peter does not teach an absolute obedience of the wife to her husband. It does teach that they are to live together in harmony with both of them submitting to God and His Word. This does not preclude there being an order within the relationship, but it certainly precludes either partner lording it over the other.

Having looked at this passage we are now ready to look at the 'difficult passages'. Before we begin to look at these passages I want to reiterate what has already been stated.

The New Testament contains a record both of doctrine and of practice. The practice normally comes out of doctrine — however, there were times when the doctrine was 'compromised' by their practice in order to achieve a specific goal. We gave the example of Paul circumcising Timothy so as not to cause offence. So whenever we find a conflict over the practice within the New Testament and the teaching, we must always give primary weight to the teaching.

F. F. Bruce follows a similar line of argument when he discusses how we can distinguish between elements in Paul's letters which are of local and temporary application and those which are of universal and permanent validity. He says the reliable rule of thumb is 'whatever in Paul's teaching promotes true freedom is of universal and permanent validity; whatever seems to impose restrictions on true freedom has regard to local and temporary conditions'. He states that we should not turn what were meant as guiding lines for worshippers in one situation, into binding laws for all time. [1]

In that same publication Olive Rogers points out that 'it is always unwise to base Christian practice on corrective passages in the New Testament'. She states that we are on far safer ground when we base our practices on the positive statements. After then quoting Galations 3:28 'there is neither Jew nor Greek, neither slave nor free, neither male nor female, for you are all one in Christ Jesus', she concludes by saying, 'No one in our churches are barred from leadership on the grounds of racial or social discrimination, thank God! As the prejudice of the centuries has been overcome in these matters, it will surely also be overcome in the matter of equality of the sexes in the area of leadership in the church.' [2]

I believe that we have already shown that men and women are equally redeemed and so are equally eligible to serve. Theologically, that is simply saying that the New Testament teaches the priesthood of all believers (not just of all males). If these so-called 'difficult passages' show something else occurred in practice, we would still need to subordinate that to the doctrinal teaching of the New

Testament on the priesthood of all believers.

We are now ready to look at the teaching which Paul gave in these passages. We will start with the two passages in 1 Corinthians and finish this chapter with a look at the Timothy passage.

My method will be to give an exegesis of the passage in some detail and then to follow this up with a summary of the exegesis and a conclusion. Those who do not wish to go through the passage in detail might find it easier to go to the summary and conclusion first. They can then follow this up with the more detailed exegesis if they desire.

4.2 1 Corinthians 11:2–16—The question of head-covering

This is a very difficult passage to understand as there are a number of questions which we are unable to answer due to a lack of available information. In our discussions so far we have sought to answer the questions regarding the meaning of *kephale* and to whom Paul is referring when he initially talks of 'man' and 'woman' in verse 3 (see above discussion in Chapter 3: The Meaning of *Kephale*).

We may find it difficult (if not impossible) to understand the custom to which Paul refers throughout this passage. It may concern some sort of veiling or head-covering but we have no external evidence which is of any great help to us with regard to this. James Hurley puts forward the suggestion that it is not to do with head-covering but how the hair was worn—whether it was 'loosed' (*akatalyptos*) or 'unloosed' (*katakalypto*). [3] There is a background in the LXX for this but we certainly cannot be dogmatic, although it is a very attractive proposition.

There are other passages where Paul and Peter comment on the way that the women should wear their hair in worship, so Hurley's suggestion might well be pointing us in the right direction (see 1 Tim. 2:9 'to dress modestly. . . not with braided hair. . .'; 1 Pet. 3:3 'your beauty should not come from outward adornment, such as braided hair . . .'). It also needs to be noted that if the women were in the custom of wearing a veil this would in fact obscure their hair and so render obsolete any instruction on how the hair should be worn.

Indeed the word 'veil'(NIV: 'covering') is only used in verse 15 where he says that long hair is given to the woman 'instead of' (Greek *anti*) a veil. It is, however, possible that the word *anti* is being used here in the sense of equivalence and could be simply translated, as in the NIV, by the word 'as '.

When we place the various points together, it seems not improbable that Paul is simply talking about men and women presenting their hair differently, rather than putting forward some doctrine of head-covering.

Another plausible proposal is that the veil was worn by the married women to show that they were unavailable, and that it was the sign that they had authority in themselves. This would be meaning that when they were veiled, they had equal rights to pray and prophesy alongside the men.

It is true that the exact custom outlined here cannot be determined and we can only assume that the custom itself is not an issue which God wants us to be concerned about. I do believe, though, that there is an underlying principle being expressed which is unchanging. If we accept that the outworking of this underlying principle will be cultural, we are then left with the important issue of discovering the underlying principle itself. We might then want to express this underlying principle in an appropriate way within our own culture.

4.2.1 A brief exegesis of the passage

Paul begins in verse 2 with, 'I praise you for remembering me in everything.' He commends them for holding to the tradition or teaching that he had passed on. If we contrast this with verse 17, where he cannot commend them for their disorder over the Lord's Supper, it would lead us to believe that Paul is generally approving of their conduct in this passage which we are currently looking at.

What then is the tradition which he approves of? It is unlikely that it is the issue of head-covering, as it would appear from the passage that he is bringing correction and clarification on that matter, so it would not be easy to see how Paul could be approving of their conduct on the one hand and then bringing correction to it on the other. This would leave us with the distinct possibility that the tradition that he commends them in following is that of the equality of the sexes before God—as is evidenced by the fact that they are allowing men and women to prophesy.

As the passage unfolds, I believe we will see that the Corinthians were very keen to defend this equality—so keen in fact that they inadvertently undermined the teaching which Paul had passed on to them.

Having begun with a commendation, he then has to bring some adjustment because the Corinthians were taking the equality of the sexes to a point where they were losing the distinction between the genders. So he begins verse 3 with the words, 'Now I want you to understand . . . ' He is going to lay a foundation here which will enable him to bring in some correction.

He has commended them but he now wants to bring some clarification to the outworking of the teaching, so he brings in a new element through saying in effect 'but I also want you to realise that there is headship'.

There are two possibilities that Paul is setting out here: one is that he is describing a hierarchy (God—Christ—husband—wife), or secondly that Paul is illustrating headship by taking three different relationships, all of which contain the principle of headship. If Paul is seeking to describe a hierarchy, it seems strange that he sought to obscure this by beginning with the middle relationship within this hierarchy rather than at one end or the other. It is therefore better to take it that he is setting out the three relationships as three different illustrations of the same principle of headship. This fits in better with the passage as a whole, when we consider the central theme to be the headship of the husband in relation to his wife and how this should affect their approach to God in worship.

Paul places this headship relationship (husband–wife) alongside two others and therefore shows that he did not view the headship of the man in relation to his wife as a purely temporal or cultural issue. (See Chapter 3: The

Meaning of *Kephale* —for the reasons why I believe this is husband–wife and not simply man–woman.) Although I would limit what he is saying on headship here to marriage, it would seem clear that he broadens the words to mean male and female in later verses (e.g. v. 12). We also need to remember the custom was for the women to be married or to remain under the authority of their fathers, so Paul would not have found it so necessary in his culture to address the single women. We will see this illustrated in 1 Corinthians 14:35 where the women are told to ask their husbands at home. In that context it is evident that Paul does not deal with single women as a separate group as, in a very real sense, they did not exist as an independent group within that culture.

We also need to determine what Paul is seeking to achieve by using the headship argument. It is clear that he is not wanting to put forward that women are inferior to men—he accepts throughout the passage that there is an equality of function. In addition, if there was an inferiority, we would also need to apply this to the relationship of Christ to God. I believe it leaves us the option that headship implies order and distinctiveness in a way that does not in itself deny equality.

If we follow some of Paul's arguments through, I believe it will point us in this direction. A central theme in this passage is dishonour and honour. A woman being a woman (as expressed through her hair) is her glory (v.15)—it brings honour to herself. She is created as a woman and when the inner contentment and self-acceptance shines through it is very fitting. It will bring honour to herself and to womanhood. It will also bring honour to her husband (v.7)—it will put him in his right setting. A man presenting himself as a man will honour himself and his gender and in turn bring honour to Christ (cf. v.4—a man dishonouring his head) and also to God (man is the glory of God, v.7).

So when men and women seek to express themselves as men and women without competing with each other, they will bring glory to God. Paul argues very strongly against a form of feminism where the women need to act and present themselves as a man would. A woman is not to be man in a woman's body—rather the Gospel liberates women to be women and frees them to function as women alongside men without feeling inferior.

His argument is based on headship (order and distinctiveness) and that a husband and wife relate together within that order—this is a creation order which does not imply inequality. However, this might lead some to believe that he therefore expected a clear subordination of women to men in their functions in the body. To cover this he says in verse 11 that 'in the Lord' there is total interdependence. So the order is in the horizontal relationship as expressed in marriage—this needs to be expressed in a suitable cultural way showing women to be women and men to be men. Vertically, and therefore functionally in the body, there is total equality but this equality does not mean that we can seek to obliterate the distinctiveness of the genders.

In verses 4 to 6 Paul goes on to accept that men and women will have equal opportunity to pray and to prophesy. They had equal rights before God although he argues in favour of differing customs in terms of their hair.

It seems better to take the word 'head' as literal throughout these verses when it is used in connection with hair, and probably in both the literal and metaphorical sense when it talks about dishonouring. Paul is then saying for a woman to present herself physically as a man would (expressed in the way she wears her hair) is to dishonour herself ('her head' i.e. her womanhood) and also her husband as 'her head' and the marriage relationship. If a man was to do the reverse, that is to present himself physically as a woman would, then he too would be dishonouring himself and Christ ('his head'). So for a woman to dress her hair as a man would is not in fact a declaration of her freedom, rather it is a dishonouring of her gender and a denial of her freedom. A woman is free to pray and to prophesy as a woman and a man is free to do so as a man.

One could understand this problem arising among the women who believed they were now as free as any man to express themselves in Christ. If they were equal before

God, why should they not show how free and equal they were by also demonstrating culturally that they were free, by wearing their hair in the same way as the men did? Paul's response in effect was—you are free to pray and prophesy as a woman; in fact by denying your femininity you are not expressing your freedom as a woman, but are actually denying it. For a woman to do this would actually mean that she was dishonouring herself and bringing shame on herself (not dissimilar to the shame that prostitutes brought on womanhood—if this is the reference to being shorn which Paul makes here in verse 6).

Paul then goes on to use arguments based in the creation narratives (verses 7 to 9) to back up his point that men and women are different. Equality to express themselves does not mean that men and women are identical. They were created to be different and this difference is not to be done away with, as this would be a denial of God's original creative act.

To try to bring out a superiority of the male over the female from these verses is to draw out something which is not in Genesis. This has led some (e.g. G.B. Caird [4]) to accuse Paul of faulty exegesis. It would seem that Paul is simply emphasising that there are creation differences and a woman does not need to imitate a man but can worship freely as a woman.

To suggest that Paul is saying that woman is only in the image of God in a secondary sense (verse 7) is to go against the teaching of Genesis 1:26 and the explicit revelation that all mankind (male and female) are united either in Adam or in Christ. Paul avoids this position by not quoting directly from Genesis (he uses 'image and glory' not 'image and likeness'). Further, he does not say that woman is the image of man—simply that she is the glory of man. It is probably best to take this word 'glory' to mean 'bring honour to', as Paul says what brings honour to a woman is her hair (see verse 15 'her hair is her glory'). A man is there to reflect God and bring honour to Him by being a man, and a woman will further bring honour to man (or perhaps her man) by expressing her own femininity. This will honour her man and so also bring honour to God.

In verse 10 Paul says, 'For this reason, the woman ought to have ... authority over (or on) her head.' Whatever the exact meaning is here it is clearly referring to the woman having authority herself. The Greek phrase does not mean that she is to be under authority, but must be taken to mean that she has power to exercise her authority or her rights. When she complies with whatever is being asked of her (head-covering or having her hair done in an appropriate way, etc.) she is able to act with authority. Her authority on or over her head is in fact then to be seen as her right to function.

There is a diversity of opinion over the phrase 'because of the angels'. Probably the simplest explanation is that the angels are respecters of the created order and so must we be. Women are to respect the fact that God has created them as women and men are to respect the fact that they have been created as men.

Verses 11 and 12 begin with Paul stating that in the Lord there is a clear interdependence between the man and the woman. They are each dependent on one another and both are dependent on God. In creation there was a dependence of woman on the man in terms of origin, but since the original creation every man now comes into the world through woman, so even in terms of natural life there is a mutual dependence.

Paul then returns to the issue in hand in verses 13 to 15. He argues how right and fitting it is for a woman to have her hair done appropriately—his final appeal being to what they 'feel' is right. He says this is 'the very nature of things'. Then in verse 15 he finally argues against veiling (her long hair is given to her instead of a veil) or possibly to the fact that as she is veiled already (by her long hair) it is only right that she should wear a veil. This latter suggestion would take *anti* to mean 'as '—nature veils a woman so we should accept it as right. I would prefer the former position with Paul actually arguing against veiling.

This passage ends in verse 16 where Paul says that they have no such (*toiauten*) practice nor do any of the other churches. What is the practice which he is referring to? It is perfectly possible that he is saying they have no such practice as veiling (taking verse 15 as 'long hair' instead of a 'veil'), or that this is referring to the passage as a whole, and Paul is saying that there is no such practice in any church as seeking to blur the distinctions between the sexes. The men can worship God in freedom as men and the women can freely worship God as women.

4.2.2 Summary of the exegesis

1. They had done well in holding to the teaching/ tradition which Paul had passed on to them. This was his teaching that the sexes were equal before God—all believers were part of the new covenant priesthood.
2. However, this equality does not mean that there are now no differences—in fact far from it. He draws initially on the principle of headship as the basis for his argument. Headship means that there is order and distinctiveness.
3. Men and women have an equal role in expressing themselves in prayer and prophecy, but equality does not mean identity. They are equal before God but not identical to each other—creation tells us this.
4. This distinction needs to be respected in the same way as the angels respect the created order.
5. In Christ there is mutual dependence—this can be seen in the areas of creation and procreation. Even then we recognise that all life proceeds from God.
6. There should also be no covering of the woman's hair by a veil—quite the opposite as the truth is that her hair has been given to her instead of a veil and is her glory.
7. There is no such practice as veiling anywhere in the churches. (Or perhaps he is summarising the passage and saying—there is no practice of blurring the distinctions between the sexes.)

4.2.3 Conclusions

I suggest that the context in which Paul is addressing the problem was one where they were worried that if they followed conventional and cultural custom, they would end up denying the equality of the sexes. He points out that equality does not imply a necessity of identification and therefore there is no need to overthrow any convention in dress which emphasises this distinction. In fact to do so is to say that men are superior and that women are not free to function unless they become like men. So breaking with convention would in fact be a denial of the freedom the Gospel brings.

The Gospel liberates women as women—they have nothing to prove so are to pray and prophesy portraying themselves as women. Indeed if they break with custom (through how they wear their hair) they would be denying the very freedom the Gospel brings.

So I believe, far from limiting women in function, Paul is commending them for functioning on an equal basis to the men. He simply indicates that they had been in danger of inadvertently undermining and denying this equality through their desire to express it outwardly. Women are to get on and function as women, men as men. The Gospel message is the basis for this freedom and there is no need to seek to prove it through denying the distinctiveness of the sexes.

4.3 1 Corinthians 14:34–36—Women to be silent

'Women should remain silent in the churches.' This statement of Paul's needs to be taken in context if we are going to understand exactly what he is meaning at this point. An illustration might help to underline the need for us to see these verses in their context. In a classroom situation a teacher might well say to one of the children, 'Be quiet, you are not allowed to talk in class', if the child was talking out of turn and creating a disturbance. If later the teacher were to ask the same child a question, we would be very surprised if he refused to answer it on the basis of the teacher's rebuke, which was meant to cover a specific situation.

I believe the situation which Paul describes here is a very close parallel to the illustration given. However, a number of other solutions have been given, one of which I will outline below.

There is the suggestion that these verses were a quote from the Judaisers with which Paul clearly disagrees in his reply in verses 36 to 38. This would fit in with the statement 'as the Law says' which would then be the Jewish oral law.

If this is not a quote, we first of all need to state that it cannot be an absolute prohibition against women speaking in the church—otherwise there is a clear conflict with chapter 11 verse 5 where women are allowed to pray and to prophesy. Even in this chapter he has earlier stated that when they come together each one comes with a hymn, a word of instruction etc.—he gave no indication that the women are excluded from this.

So the silence needs to be qualified in the light of what we already know is allowed. In other words it must be referring to a particular type of speaking which is prohibited. I believe it will become clear that Paul is now giving instruction with regard to this particular type of speaking.

The Greek verb *sigao* (to be silent) has already been used in this chapter. Paul used it in connection with a person speaking in a tongue (verse 28) and in connection with a prophet speaking (verse 30). There was no absolute prohibition against speaking in tongues nor against prophesying (quite the opposite in fact) but Paul did want everything to be done in an orderly fashion. I suggest the prohibition against women speaking is in the same category as the prohibition against the speaker in tongues and the prophet. There is a remarkable similarity between the three prohibitions which we will outline below.

In all three situations those speaking are bringing disorder, so Paul commands the situation to stop by the speaker becoming silent and then he gives an alternative which will answer the problem and maintain order.

The first situation is of a person speaking in tongues where there is no interpreter (the problem). Paul says the speaker in tongues is to be silent (the command to bring order) and is to speak to himself and to God (the alternative).

The second situation is of a prophet speaking under

inspiration of the Holy Spirit and not giving room to others (hence his plea 'the spirits of prophets are subject to the control of prophets', v.32). This then was the problem. He says let the first prophet be silent (the command to bring order) and let the second one carry on so as all can be instructed (the alternative).

The third situation follows a parallel pattern. Again there is a situation which is disorderly—women are asking questions publicly which is distracting (the problem). Paul says that they need to be silent on this matter (his command to bring order) and that they need to ask their questions at home to their own husbands (the alternative).

This interpretation fits the context well, which is of order within worship—'everything should be done in a fitting and orderly way' (verse 40). The above interpretation has answered the basic question regarding what the area of disorder was that Paul is addressing here. From the passage it would appear that the disorder was of women calling out publicly for answers to their questions. This was a great distraction and on this matter they needed to be silent and in submission. I suggest that this submission is not here to their husbands or to men, but to the assembled body of believers.

The issue of women speaking out of turn can be illustrated from two more modern situations. Leroy Birney originally published a paper in 1971 called 'The role of women in the New Testament church' and added a postscript to it in 1979. In the postscript he writes, 'For example, I would no longer reject out-of-hand the possibility that the problem was women shouting across the aisle to ask their husbands questions since I have seen similar interruptions in new churches in Colombia.' [5]

Another example is to be found in the experience of James McKeown in his work in Ghana. Within that culture (where the women are very much seen as second class) he discovered that, if the women were not told that they had come to a meeting to learn, then they would simply gossip and chatter among themselves. [6]

Although we might only be able to surmise as to what the actual disturbances were, it seems to be most probable that the situation that Paul is addressing is of women who were causing a major disturbance, to which he needed to bring order.

It is unclear whether the rebuke of verse 36 ('Did the word of God originate with you? Or are you the only people it has reached?') is attached to the statement on women or to the overall theme of these chapters and the need for order within worship. In the light of the fact that verses 34 and 35 are placed after verse 40 in some manuscripts, it would appear better to apply verse 36 to the overall passage and not just to these verses on women.

4.3.1 Summary and conclusion

Paul is not giving an edict which is absolute, rather he is giving direction over a situation which was causing disorder in the worship. He says it is inappropriate for women to call out in the midst of a flow of the Holy Spirit. That is not the time for them to make their enquiries—they should rather remain silent and ask their husbands at home. He is not discouraging them from learning—in fact he is encouraging them to learn. He actually gives a command 'let them enquire'. So he is encouraging the women to learn but has to bring appropriate order to the situation.

4.4 1 Timothy 2:11–15—Women are not allowed to teach

This passage raises a number of questions which need to be answered. At the outset, we can say that this prohibition cannot be an absolute command against all women teaching at all times and in all contexts. I believe we can show this to be the case by listing certain points below:

1. Timothy travelled with Paul and would have been well acquainted with Paul's teaching. If Paul never allowed women to teach, why would he have been so unclear that he did allow them to teach at Ephesus? (This needs to be borne in mind as well by those who maintain women are allowed to teach women but not to teach men.)

2. Paul himself encouraged women to teach children and other women (Titus 2:3–5; 2 Tim. 1:5; 3:14). We know from those encouragements that the prohibition on teaching cannot be absolute. (This also gives considerable weight to the argument that Paul is giving one prohibition in verse 11 and not two separate ones—i.e. any prohibition against women teaching is qualified. Here it is qualified by describing the manner of the teaching—with a domineering attitude.)

If women are barred from teaching because they are prone to deception (an argument drawn by some from verse 14) it is rather surprising that Paul allows them to teach other women and children. In fact, one could argue that women and children would need to be taught by someone who could teach very clearly and accurately—which would surely disqualify someone who was prone to deception. It is also rather ironic when Paul indicates that the qualities present in Timothy's life were due mainly to the input of godly women—his mother and grandmother (2 Tim.3:15;1:5)!

3. Women are allowed to prophesy, which often includes inspired instruction, so why are they not allowed to instruct in other ways? Prophecy and teaching both need to be weighed against revealed truth. We cannot argue that prophecy was to be judged but that the teacher was allowed to teach authoritatively without any checks and balances.

4. At least one woman associated with Paul was involved in teaching a man. (Acts 18:26—Priscilla teaching Apollos with her husband Aquila. Some believe that Priscilla had the main role in this team ministry.)

5. Outside of Paul's letters, we know from Revelation 2:20–23 that there was a woman called Jezebel who taught. The church at Thyatira is not rebuked for allowing her to teach because she was a woman. The church is, however, rebuked because they did not bring discipline to the woman over the means, effect and content of her teaching. This would have been equally true if she had been a man. The

problem was not who was doing the teaching but what was being taught.

Now we know that the prohibition cannot be absolute, we need to look at ways in which this passage will harmonise with the rest of Paul's teaching—and, indeed, with the rest of Scripture.

4.4.1 Possible solutions to the situation at Ephesus

4.4.1.1 We are dealing with a Gnostic background and specifically an Eve-cult

There may be some evidence of a Gnostic-type heresy at Ephesus. For instance, Paul tells Timothy to guard what had been entrusted to his care and to turn away from godless chatter and the opposing ideas which are falsely called knowledge (Greek *gnosis*). The Gnostics, of course, claimed to have received special secret knowledge through revelation (see 1 Tim. 6:20).

The Gnostics taught that there were many mediators between God and man. Paul, however, emphatically states in 1 Timothy 2:5 that there is only one mediator between God and man, the man Christ Jesus. Gnostics offered special knowledge—Paul says it is through Christ that we come to a knowledge of the truth.

If Gnosticism is involved here, then it would be of an early, incipient type and, if this is so, we have very little material to suggest exactly what its tenets were. Trombley, in his book *Who Said Women Can't Teach?* follows the argument put forward by Catherine Kroeger that this is an Eve-cult. The argument draws on a number of points from the context, some of which we will list below, together with Paul's response to them.

1. These women promised godliness to their disciples (v. 10 the Greek verb *epangello* normally means 'to promise'—translated as 'profess' in the NIV). They believed that Eve had received special knowledge and revelation which they could pass on. Paul answers this by saying that, far from Eve receiving special knowledge, she had, in fact, been deceived.

2. These Gnostic women were using their sexual attractiveness to seduce their male disciples. This is drawn from a possible interpretation of the word *authentein* (NIV 'have authority'). This word was used at a later date to describe the latest techniques of a prostitute in enticing men. Paul counters this by saying that they are not to entice men and are to dress modestly (1 Tim. 2:9). (For a further discussion on the meaning of the word *authentein,* see below under 'Note on the use of the word *authentein'.*)

3. They believed Eve was created first—Paul clearly states that this was not the case.

Comments on this proposal
With regard to Gnosticism as a background, we conclude that there is possibly a Gnostic-type heresy which is beginning to develop here. However, there is no firm evidence as to what exactly it was and therefore how this would affect our exegesis of the role of women as outlined here by Paul.

It also needs to be noted that the teaching that was causing problems probably came from both men and women. We can certainly say that it was not being propagated only by the women. (See 1 Timothy 1:3 where the generic term *tis* is used. This should be translated as 'certain people': NIV 'certain men').

Excursus: note on the use of the word authentein
Paul's normal word for 'authority' is *exousia* which he does not use here. In fact, this is the only occurrence of this word in the New Testament. There are two possible ways of explaining the meaning of this word. As suggested above, the word did come to describe the latest techniques of a prostitute in enticing men. This meaning however appears to be later than the usage in New Testament times. If it did mean this, it would fit in well with Paul's appeal for the women to dress modestly.

The other possible meaning is drawn from the noun to which this verb is related. This noun had a meaning of suicide or murder, particularly within the family. So the verb carried the meaning of 'self-willed behaviour'. Anderson comments on this passage, 'It is not the question of instructing or teaching him but the manner of doing it' which is in question in these verses.[7]

Paul, in choosing this rare word, must be seeking to communicate something more than 'have authority over'. He uses the normal Greek word for 'have authority over' in 1 Corinthians 7:4 (Greek *exousiazo*). There he says that, within the marriage relationship, the husband has authority over the wife's body and likewise the woman has authority over his body. So the authority is mutual and equal within the marriage relationship, at least as far as the sexual relationship is concerned. If all Paul wanted to communicate was 'have authority over' he would not have used this word *authentein*.

It would seem that the best translation is probably that of domineering—so meaning a very strong type of authority. However we translate, it would seem important to communicate this sense of self-willed behaviour—an attitude of 'no one will tell me what to do!'

We also know that Ephesus was a centre for the worship of the goddess Artemis (Acts 19:23–41). F.F. Bruce says that she was, in origin, the ancient goddess of Asia Minor, long worshipped in that land as the mother of gods and men. The worship was heavily sensual, presided over by eunuch-priests and three grades of priestesses.[8] This, then, was a manifestation of one of the prevailing principalities over Ephesus, so it is not surprising that Paul has to address the issue of women dressing appropriately.

Given this background, we can surmise that women who tended towards domineering their husbands were a real problem in Ephesus. If we add to this the fact that the Gospel brought liberation to the women through the priesthood of all believers, we can only assume that Timothy faced problems from some domineering women.

Having put forward that this word means to domineer over someone (perhaps even to verbally assassinate someone) we are now ready to look at two other solutions. These are two very similar proposals—one of which I will favour more than the other.

4.4.1.2 *The problem was that uneducated women were teaching*

If we consider the immediate context into which these verses fit, we see that Paul is giving instructions on how the men and the women are to conduct themselves in worship. The men are to pray lifting up holy hands, the women are to pray dressed appropriately. (The verb 'to pray' is supplied from verse 8, which is a normal Greek construction. The Greek says, 'I want the men to pray . . . likewise the women . . .'.)

Paul then gives further instructions with regard to women in the verses in question.

Firstly, he gives an instruction—the Greek is in the imperative or command mood; so the sense is 'a woman let her learn'. This was a very radical command in that society. With regard to the rest of the passage, we need to decide if Paul is giving reasons why women are to learn, or reasons why they are not to teach and have authority over men.

I take it that the former is the context in which the passage is to be understood. The verb with regard to learning is in the command form but the prohibition against teaching is in the indicative mood (denoting a simple statement of fact). I would therefore take the statements given in verses 13 to 15 to be reasons why a woman should learn and not as reasons why she is not to teach.

She is to learn with certain attitudes—quietness and full submission (a word relating to order: 'to be arranged under something'). This submission is not explained here. It is probably better to take it to mean submission to the church rather than to her husband or a man—as the context is clearly one where the church is meeting together.

Paul then continues in verse 12, saying, in effect, that he is not allowing a woman to be teaching and to be domineering over a man. He could have used much stronger language if he were insisting on a ban for all time: for example he could have used the word 'never' or used the common Greek word *dei* ('it is binding') to indicate that he was meaning a very strong prohibition against women teaching. All he uses is the Greek indicative, which simply states what his practice was.

We also need to decide if Paul is giving one or two separate prohibitions. If it is two prohibitions, then a woman is not allowed to teach, nor is she allowed to domineer over a man. If it is simply one prohibition then it is not a woman teaching which is the problem, but the manner in which she is teaching. I consider it is far better to take this as one prohibition, rather than two separate ones, for the following reasons:

1. They are better taken together in the light of the parallels which Paul has outlined here. This was a very common style among the biblical writers. Here the parallels are by way of contrast—the woman is not to teach (vocally) with a domineering attitude but is to learn quietly with a submissive attitude. So he contrasts learning with a certain attitude (submission) and teaching with a certain attitude (domineering).
2. If there was a ban on women teaching we would need to ask—why, if he had known Paul's position on this matter, did Timothy allow this in the first place? We need to remember that he was a member of Paul's apostolic team and so would have known the position Paul took on these matters.
3. We have also noted above that Paul did allow certain women to teach (see the introductory comments on this passage).

So, for the above reasons, I do not believe that Paul is giving us two prohibitions here, but one. Having sought to answer this very important point, we can now look at the remainder of verse 12.

Paul carries on with the strong negative (*alla*: but) in order to pick up the original command again. (This is known as the 'resumptive use' of the word *alla* . It was used in this way to bring the reader back to the point of immediate interest. So Paul is saying that the point in question is the command for women to learn, not the prohibition against teaching which he has just given.)

The NIV then translates this part of the verse very badly

with 'she must be silent'. The word translated 'silent' (Greek *hesuchia*) is the same word translated 'quietness' in verse 11. It is a noun which refers to the respect and order which needs to be given in a situation. It does not refer to absolute silence; for instance in 2 Thessalonians 3:12 it is translated as 'settle down'. So it would appear that he is using this word here to pick up on the original command. He is in effect saying, 'I do not allow a woman to domineer over a man, but I do allow her (to learn) in quietness'. It appears from the use of *alla* and the repetition of *hesuchia* that he is effectively putting the first half of verse 12 in parentheses. (There were no actual parenthesis marks in Greek, so they had to use an alternative, as Paul has here.)

This does not mean that we can ignore Paul's statements regarding women and teaching but that the explanations which follow in verses 13 to 15 must be seen as reasons why a woman is commanded to learn, and not as reasons why she is to be restricted in ministry.

The current solution that we are looking at is one where Timothy was facing a situation of uneducated women who were teaching. This then would mean that Paul did not allow those women to teach but he did encourage them to learn—once they had been taught they could then teach others.

I am not in favour of this argument as it stands for the following reason. The Gospel comes to liberate all mankind but it seems unlikely to me that these women, who were uneducated and downtrodden in life, were transformed in such a way that they came into the assembled body and then exerted authority. We would also need to ask why Paul only mentions the uneducated women and not also the uneducated men in this context. This leads me on to the next suggested solution, which is the one that I favour.

4.4.1.3 The problem women were women of high social standing

The exegesis of verses 11 to 12 follows the line suggested above under the suggestion regarding uneducated women. The difference in explanation is that the women who are causing the problems are women who come from a high social background. The reasons Paul gives in verses 13 to 15 are seen as reasons why a woman is to learn, and the exegesis of these verses will be the same for both of these suggested solutions.

I have already stated my reason for not accepting the previous solution. I believe the present solution is more likely when we consider the picture it would give us. These women of high social standing would have had slaves and so would have been used to exerting their wills in situations and communicating publicly. Many of them could be described as the successful businesswomen of their day. This would mean that these women had not in fact been downtrodden (unlike many of the other women of their day). They would have taken on positions of authority and probably, to a great extent, were unchallenged.

I believe this possibility is more likely than the previous one, where it was suggested that the reference was simply to uneducated women who came in and exerted themselves. This would be more likely with women who already knew how to handle positions of authority and simply carried on doing so when they came into church life. The preceding verses, which refer to women who can afford to dress themselves with gold, pearls and expensive clothes, would further point us in this direction (1 Tim. 2:9,10).

When the Gospel reached these women, they were brought into the community. When they came in, Timothy faced problems with some of them as they exerted their authority without submitting to the body. They might have been educated as far as the world went but they were uneducated with regard to the Gospel. In this context Paul is saying, using the Greek imperative,'let the women learn'.

Having laid out the situation as I see it, we can now press on and look at the remaining verses. We have already stated that these verses contain reasons why women were encouraged to learn rather than reasons why women are not allowed to teach.

Paul gives three reasons why the women were to learn. He draws his arguments from three different areas: creation, the Fall and redemption. Paul argues from Genesis, so it is important that we do not read into this passage anything which was not originally intended in Genesis.

Reason 1: from creation. In creation, Eve is equally part of God's created act, so she is not to be excluded from being taught. The creation of mankind was not finished with the creation of the male; woman was also included, so education should not stop with the male either. (Paul says Adam was formed first, *then* Eve—indicating the inclusiveness of Eve as part of God's creation of the human race; he does not say 'Adam was formed first, *not* Eve'—indicating some priority of Adam over Eve.)

Reason 2: from the Fall. Eve was totally deceived. The only answer to deception is to 'let them learn'. It is also possible that Paul is alluding to the fact that Eve was created after the explicit instruction about not eating from the tree of the knowledge of good and evil and, because she was inadequately educated, became deceived. Whether this is the case or not, she needs to be educated. In the Fall she was deceived and as truth is the only answer to deception, Paul says let her learn.

Reason 3: through redemption. In redemption the Saviour is described as the seed of woman (footnote to Gen. 3:15) so she is not to be excluded from education. She is a full member of the redeemed community and is equally redeemed along with men. She (NB the Greek of verse 15 is 'she', singular) will be saved through the childbearing—referring to Eve, as representative woman, being restored to the original state; this salvation is then open to all women (not now simply referring to Eve but to women in general as Paul changes from the singular to the plural: if they remain in faith, love and holiness with propriety—a reference back to verses 9 to10 where Paul uses the same Greek word translated here as 'propriety').

So there are three reasons why a woman is to be encouraged to learn:

1. She is part of the creation of mankind so do not exclude her from learning.
2. She fell through deception; the answer to deception

is accurate education, so that she has a full knowledge of the truth.

3. She is included in redemption and is no longer seen as a transgressor, so we need to allow her to learn.

4.4.2 Summary and conclusion

1. It is not a prohibition against all women teaching at all times.
2. It is not simply a prohibition against teaching, but against the manner in which it was carried out.
3. The thrust of the passage is that Paul wants the women to learn.
4. Timothy was facing a particular problem in Ephesus. There are certain possible explanations as to what the problem was. I favour the suggestion that women of high social standing were coming into the church community and, as a result of their cultural background, were actually teaching and domineering over men. They were lording it over them with an attitude which said 'you won't tell me what to do'. They had a lack of respect for those in authority, many of whom probably came from more humble backgrounds than themselves. Whatever education they had received they were unlearned as far as the Gospel and Scripture went.
5. Paul wants all women to learn and gives three reasons why they should—one from creation, one from the Fall and one from redemption.
6. In the midst of this, he addresses the situation in which Timothy finds himself with these women, by saying that women are not allowed to teach and domineer over men.
7. We could summarise it in this way: Paul gives a command, saying 'let a woman learn', he gives three reasons why women ought to learn and in the midst of this he gives a practical piece of advice which was his own practice. This piece of advice included a practical test—when she teaches, is she domineering over a man (possibly her husband)? (This word *authentein* must mean more than 'having authority

over' as it is such a rare use.) So Paul is not forbidding women to teach, but he does forbid women to teach in this way. This was evidently a problem in Ephesus —perhaps the women were more open to this due to the worship of the goddess Artemis which was prevalent in the area.

---

1. Bruce, F.F., 'Women in the church: a biblical survey', *Christian Brethren Review Journal*, No. 33, page 11.
2. Rogers, Olive, 'The role of women in the church', ibid., page 67.
3. Hurley, James, *Man and Woman in Biblical Perspective* (IVP, London, 1981) pages 162–184.
4. Caird, G.B., *Principalities and Powers* (Clarendon, Oxford, 1956) pages 17–22.
5. Birney, Leroy, 'The role of women in the New Testament church', *Christian Brethren Review Journal*, No. 33. The article is on pages 15–32 and this quote is found on page 30.
6. Leonard, Christine, *A Giant in Ghana* (New Wine Press, 1989) page 109.
7. Anderson, J.A., 'Woman's warfare and ministry', *Christian Herald*, London, 1935, page 30.
8. Bruce, F. F., *The Book of Acts* (Eerdmans, New International Commentary Series, 1975) pages 397, 398.

CHAPTER 5

QUESTIONS, OBSERVATIONS AND CONCLUSIONS

5.1 What about the male imagery of God in the Bible?

God is spirit and therefore is neither male nor female in our sense of this word. (It could be argued that God is both male and female from Genesis 1:27—but remember we are made in His image not He in ours.) The concept which is central to Scripture is of God being Father. This is not to be understood in simple male terms—it is a description of a relationship and role which God takes up in the lives of His people and not a description of His maleness.

There are other pictures of God which can be taken to show that He also carries out roles which are attributed to women. He is seen as providing food, water and clothing for His people. All were seen as the role of a woman within the culture to which these images were addressed.

In Numbers 11:12 we even have Moses saying by implication that God is the mother of Israel. Again in Isaiah 66:13 God speaks of comforting His people as a mother comforts a child. It is interesting, in this context, to note also that Paul in 1 Thessalonians 2:7 speaks of his apostolic work as caring for the new converts in the way a mother cares for her children. The love of God is not simply the love of a father but also that of a mother. So, while we need to hold firmly to the revealed fact that He is our Father, it is not true to say that the male imagery of God points us in the direction of the superiority of the male.

5.2 Does God use a woman if He can't find a man?

There is a proverb which says 'the exception proves the rule'. However, the exception cannot prove truth, for truth is unchanging and does not have exceptions. Women in ministry cannot end up as the exception which proves the rule. Either it is wrong for them to be in ministry, or we have established a rule which is false. So we cannot claim that God simply uses a woman when He cannot find a man, and use this as sufficient explanation for some women being involved in ministry.

In fact this claim, that God only uses a woman when He cannot find a man, has even more serious implications than if we claim that women who minister are simply the exception. In her book *Equal to Serve*, Hull deals with this by saying that, if it is wrong for God to use a woman, then it is wrong under any circumstance. Otherwise a church leadership, in the light of the fact that they had insufficient funds to finance their church programme, could say that they planned to use stolen money. If it is wrong by God's decree, then it is wrong and the ends cannot justify the means. [1]

This sort of question raises the dilemma which many people find themselves in. They recognise that God has gifted women in a specific area and that they could use those gifts to fulfil a role of ministry or leadership. If these roles are not open to them, then it begs the question of why God gifted them in this way in the first place.

5.3 Why did Jesus not choose any female apostles?

Jesus lived and ministered in the transition period between the two covenants. His actions cannot therefore be seen as setting out the boundaries of church leadership for the future. We would also need to push the question further by asking why Jesus did not choose to have some non-Jews as His apostles. The reason again is that He lived and ministered between the two covenants.

So, in answering this question, I would suggest that there was no permanent significance with regard to the future leadership of the church in Jesus only choosing males (and Jews) as His apostles. The significance seems to be that Jesus chose the twelve as the founders of His new Israel in the same way as the twelve patriarchs were the founders of the tribes of Israel (Luke 22:30). So the twelve male disciples were seen as the new order counterparts to the twelve patriarchs of the old order.

Although Jesus did not choose any women to be part of the band of twelve apostles, it is clear for all to see that Jesus treated women in a totally revolutionary way and certainly women were among those who followed Him as disciples (e.g. Luke. 8:1–3; 10:38–42).

We could also highlight the fact that women played a far more prominent role in the crucifixion and resurrection narratives than men. Here again, it would be very doubtful whether this point has any permanent significance for the ongoing life of the church.

So it would seem that the choice of twelve Jewish male apostles has no bearing on the future leadership of God's people.

5.4 What about Jesus? — He was male!

We do not know all the reasons why certain things are the way they are. We do know though that Jesus was male because He came as the last Adam. The human race is seen as either in Adam, or in Christ (the last Adam).

The fact that Jesus was male is a strong argument against that of the 'Split Image' theology—where God is only revealed in the togetherness of the male and female. Jesus, as a male, represented God fully and we, as men or women, can also represent Him fully, as we allow the Holy Spirit to transform us back into the image of Jesus.

5.5 Are any women mentioned as elders in the New Testament?

There is no woman anywhere in the New Testament who is specifically mentioned as an elder (*presbuteros*) or an overseer (*episkopos*). However, it is also true that no man is mentioned as an overseer and that the only men who are specifically referred to as elders are Peter (1 Pet. 5:1) and the writer of 2 and 3 John (who might have been the Apostle John).

We do have, however, the mention of women who apparently led house churches and also the strong possibility that the 'elect lady' of 2 John 1 was a female leader of a church. So we cannot be absolute in assuming that there were no women who were elders in New Testament times.

The teaching in the New Testament would certainly not appear in any way to limit a woman when it came to taking up any ministry or office, provided she fulfilled the necessary criteria and was anointed of God.

5.6 Should women get married or have a career?

Hull, in her book *Equal to Serve*, shows that this is an unfair question, as marriage cannot be compared to a career. Marriage is a relationship, while a career is not. They cannot therefore be placed in parallel. Nor can a person be asked to choose between the two. As Hull points out, no one would present this same question to a man.

A couple do have certain questions to answer in terms of how their careers fit in with their responsibilities within the marriage—but the choice is not between the two as outlined in the question above.

5.7 Other Observations

As far as the rights of the first-born are concerned, we have noted how God Himself overruled this in certain situations. For example, this was the case with Jacob over Esau and Ephraim over Manasseh, to mention but two instances.

With regard to a 'chain of authority', again we need to remember that Jesus promised that His sheep would hear His voice themselves. God spoke directly to Mary—He did not ask for Joseph's permission nor did He delegate Joseph to bring the message to her. God did not use a chain of command here. We need to be very careful, when we emphasise order, that we do not end up denying the fundamental truth of each believer being in personal relationship with the Good Shepherd.

Anthropos translated as 'men'. The Greek word *anthropos* (mankind) is sometimes translated, by implication, as 'male' where this is both unnecessary and unhelpful. One example would be Hebrews 13:17: 'Obey your leaders and submit to their authority. They keep watch over you as *men* who will give an account.' By implication the text reads in English as if the leaders will necessarily be male—this is not a necessary implication with the Greek text. Another example is in 2 Timothy 2:2 where Timothy is encouraged to entrust Paul's teachings to faithful *men*. Again the implication of gender in the English text is not there in the Greek.

5.8 Conclusions

I do not find in Scripture anything which could be described as a calling in God which is barred from a woman. A woman is free to fulfil any calling which God puts on her life in the same way as a man is free to fulfil his call. In order to do so, a woman is to remain feminine and so fulfil her call as a woman. She is not to act and present herself as a man would.

This position is the only viable one which enables us to maintain with integrity the universal priesthood of all believers. The 'difficult passages', when understood in their context, can be seen to be answering specific problems and need not be seen as compromising the fundamental truth of equal redemption, which gives all believers equal opportunity to serve.

Having gone through this study, I do believe that there is an order within the marriage relationship. This is not in conflict with the above freedom. It is simply recognising that home and church are two distinct spheres. We also need to bear in mind that authority and submission need to be understood in the way that is taught in the Bible.

Within the marriage there needs to be submission to Christ as Lord over the relationship. This could be called submitting as one flesh to the Lord. There also needs to be a mutual submission to one another. (All believers are required to submit to one another.) There is also the specific submission of the wife to the husband.

So let us rejoice together in the liberty and unity which the Gospel brings! If there are questions which remain, let us deal with each other graciously, knowing that God is always willing to shed more light where we are seeking answers which will help us continue to walk in integrity before Him.

My final plea is that we work together in bringing the good news of the Gospel to a world which needs to hear. In order to do that we will need the release of all those who know that God has redeemed them and are willing to lay down their lives in service of one another.

---

1. Hull, op. cit., page 42.

BIBLIOGRAPHY

Abbott-Smith, G., *Manual Greek Lexicon of the New Testament* (T. & T. Clark, 1936).

Arndt, W.F. and Gingrich, F.W., *A Greek English Lexicon of the New Testament and Other Early Christian Literature* (University of Chicago Press, 1952).

Atkins, Anne, *Split Image* (Hodder & Stoughton, 1987).

Barnett, Paul W., 'Wives and women's ministry (1 Timothy 2:11–15)', *Evangelical Quarterly*, Vol. LXI, No. 3, July 1989.

Black, Hugh B., *A Trumpet Call to Women* (New Dawn Books, 1988).

Brauch, Manfred, *Hard Sayings of Paul* (Hodder & Stoughton, 1989).

Brown, Colin (editor), *The New International Dictionary of the New Testament* (Paternoster Press; Vol. 1, 1975; Vol. 2, 1975; Vol. 3, 1978).

Bruce, F.F., *The Book of Acts* (Eerdmans, New International Commentary Series, 1975).

Cotterell, Peter, and Turner, Max, *Linguistics and Biblical Interpretation* (SPCK, 1989).

Cranfield, C.E.B., *Romans 2* (ICC Commentary Series, Edinburgh, 1975).

Ellis, E. Earle, *Pauline Theology — Ministry and Society* (Eerdmans/Paternoster, 1989).

Evans, Mary, *Woman in the Bible* (Paternoster Press, 1983).

Henderson, Arthur (editor), 'Women in the Church', *Christian Brethren Review Journal*, No. 33.

Hurley, James, *Man and Woman in Biblical Perspective* (IVP, London, 1981).

Hull, Gretchen Gaebelein, *Equal to Serve* (Scripture Union, 1989).

Morris, Leon, *The Epistle to the Romans* (Eerdmans/IVP, 1988).

Moule, C.F.D., *The Epistles to the Colossians and to Philemon* (Cambridge Greek Testament Commentary, CUP, 1968).

Padgett, Alan, 'The Pauline rationale for submission: biblical feminism and the hina clauses of Titus 2:1–10', *Evangelical Quarterly*, Vol. LIX, No.1, January 1987.

Park, David M., 'The structure of authority in marriage', *Evangelical Quarterly*, Vol. IX, No. 2, April 1987.

Pawson, David, *Leadership is Male* (Highland Books, 1988).

Robinson, J. Armitage, *St Paul's Epistle to the Ephesians* (Macmillan & Co., 1903).

Trombley, Charles, *Who Said Women Can't Teach?* (Logos, 1985).